Find It *Fast* in the Bible

Ron Rhodes

HARVEST HOUSE PUBLISHERS

EUGENE, OREGON

FIND IT FAST IN THE BIBLE
Copyright © 2000 by Ron Rhodes
Published by Harvest House Publishers
Eugene, Oregon 97402
www.harvesthousepublishers.com

ISBN 978-0-7369-2656-0

Printed in the United States of America

10 11 12 13 14 15 16 / BP-SK / 10 9 8 7 6 5 4 3 2

A

ABILITY

Can do all things through Christ—*Philippians 4:13*.
Divine source of ability—*1 Peter 4:11*.
Increased abilities through Christ—*John 14:12*.

ABORTION

God has a purpose for those in womb—*Jeremiah 1:5*.
Rights of the unborn—*Exodus 21:22,23*.
Unborn children are persons—*Psalm 51:5; 139:13-16*.
Unborn children have consciousness—*Luke 1:41,44*.

ABSTINENCE FROM LIQUOR, EXAMPLES OF

Daniel—*Daniel 1:8*.
John the Baptist—*Matthew 11:18; Luke 1:15*.
Nazirite vow—*Numbers 6:3,4*.
Samson's mother—*Judges 13:4,14*.

ACCEPTANCE

Accept all authority—*1 Peter 2:13*.
Accept both good and adversity from God—*Job 2:10*.
Accept Christians weak in faith—*Romans 14:1*.
Accept counsel—*Proverbs 4:10*.
Accept discipline—*Proverbs 19:20*.
Accept one another—*Romans 15:7*.
Accept situation Lord has put you in—*1 Corinthians 7:17*.
Wife, accept authority of husband—*1 Peter 3:1*.

ACCOMPLISHMENT

Accomplish what God calls us to—*1 Corinthians 9:24-27*.

Can accomplish anything with Christ's help—
Philippians 4:13.

Necessity of being rooted in Christ—*John 15:1-8.*

Necessity of relationship with Holy Spirit—*Galatians 5:22,23.*

ACCOUNTABILITY

For use of money—*Luke 19:15.*

For words spoken—*Matthew 12:36,37.*

In accordance with level of understanding—*1 Samuel 3:7; Luke 12:48.*

To God—*Ezekiel 18:20; Romans 3:19; 14:12.*

ACCURACY

Accurate measurement—*Isaiah 28:17.*

Every jot and tittle of Scripture accurate—*Matthew 5:17,18.*

Perfect aim—*Judges 20:16.*

Scripture words accurate—*Matthew 22:41-46.*

Singular word in Scripture accurate—*Galatians 3:16.*

Use accurate scales—*Leviticus 19:36; Deuteronomy 25:13.*

Verb tense in Scripture accurate—*Matthew 22:23-33.*

ACCUSATIONS, FALSE

Enemies say evil things—*Psalm 41:5.*

False accusations—*Luke 3:14.*

False reports—*Exodus 23:1.*

Followers of Jesus lied about—*Matthew 5:11.*

Slanderous gossip—*Leviticus 19:16.*

ADOPTION INTO GOD'S FAMILY

By faith in Christ—*Galatians 3:26.*

Father allows us into His family—*1 John 3:1,2.*

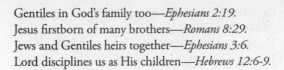

Gentiles in God's family too—*Ephesians 2:19*.
Jesus firstborn of many brothers—*Romans 8:29*.
Jews and Gentiles heirs together—*Ephesians 3:6*.
Lord disciplines us as His children—*Hebrews 12:6-9*.

ADULTERY

Abstain from sexual immorality—*Acts 15:20*.
Adulterer sins in private—*Job 24:15*.
Adultery forbidden—*Exodus 20:14*.
Adultery starts in the heart—*Matthew 15:19; Mark 7:21*.
Adultery with the eyes—*Matthew 5:28; 2 Peter 2:14*.
Avoid sexually immoral people—*1 Corinthians 5:9-11*.
Death penalty in Old Testament times—*Leviticus 20:10*.
Divorce and adultery—*Matthew 5:32*.
Keep clear of sexual sin—*Colossians 3:5*.
Make a covenant with your eyes to avoid lust—*Job 31:1*.
Sexual immorality brings judgment—*1 Corinthians 10:8*.
Sexual immorality emerges from sinful nature—
    Galatians 5:19.

ADVERSITY

All of us encounter trouble—*Job 5:7*.
Builds endurance—*Romans 5:3,4*.
Cast all anxiety on God—*Psalm 55:22; 1 Peter 5:7*.
Christ gives us rest—*Matthew 11:28*.
Christ helps us in temptation—*Hebrews 2:18*.
Count it all joy—*James 1:2*.
Do not be discouraged if God disciplines you—
    Proverbs 3:11,12; Hebrews 12:5,6.
Do not be dismayed—*Isaiah 41:10*.
Do not be troubled; trust Christ—*John 14:1*.

Do not worry, Lord will fight for you—*Exodus 14:13,14.*

Go boldly to throne of grace—*Hebrews 4:16.*

God brings consolation—*Lamentations 3:32.*

God brings good out of evil—*Genesis 50:20.*

God encourages us—*2 Corinthians 7:6.*

God gives rest to the weary—*Jeremiah 31:25.*

God heals the brokenhearted—*Psalm 147:3.*

God helps in times of trouble—*Psalm 46:1.*

God is our refuge—*Deuteronomy 33:27; Psalm 9:9.*

God of all comfort helps us—*2 Corinthians 1:3,7.*

God strengthens the weak—*Isaiah 40:29.*

God turns mourning into joy—*Jeremiah 31:13.*

God will never forsake you—*Hebrews 13:5.*

God's strength makes up for our weakness—
    2 Corinthians 12:9.

Present troubles insignificant in view of future glory—
    2 Corinthians 4:17.

Pressed, but not crushed—*2 Corinthians 4:8.*

Suffering can be good for you—*Psalm 119:71.*

Trials test our faith—*1 Peter 1:6,7.*

Trust God in times of trouble—*Psalm 50:15.*

We will not drown in deep rivers—*Isaiah 43:2.*

ADVICE

Be quick to listen—*James 1:19.*

Listen to God—*John 6:45.*

Listening makes one wise—*Proverbs 19:20.*

Obtain guidance—*Proverbs 20:18.*

Plans fail for lack of counsel—*Proverbs 15:22.*

Sheep listen to shepherd—*John 10:27*.

Son, listen to your father—*Proverbs 1:8; 13:1*.

Wise man listens—*Proverbs 12:15; 13:10*.

AFFLICTED, DUTY TO THE

Be a Good Samaritan—*Luke 10:25-37*.

Be kind to despairing friend—*Job 6:14*.

Be kind to strangers—*1 Timothy 5:10; Hebrews 13:2*.

Be sympathetic—*Philippians 2:1,2*.

Feed hungry, clothe naked, visit prisoners—*Matthew 25:31-46*.

AFFLUENCE

Accumulating wealth, meaningless—*Ecclesiastes 4:8*.

Can hinder attaining salvation—*Matthew 19:16-26*.

Do not envy the affluent—*Psalm 73:3-28*.

Do not store treasures on earth—*Matthew 6:19*.

False confidence in wealth—*Psalm 49:5-8*.

God blesses with riches, wealth, honor—*2 Chronicles 1:11,12*.

Lure of wealth—*Matthew 13:22*.

Not worth losing one's soul—*Matthew 16:26*.

Prosperity short-lived—*Psalm 37:35,36*.

Store up treasure in heaven—*Luke 12:33*.

Where your treasure is, there your heart is—*Luke 12:34*.

AGE

Be mindful of how brief life is—*Psalm 39:4,5*.

God has assigned years—*Psalm 90:10*.

God sovereign over length of life—*Job 14:5*.

Honor father and mother, live long—*Exodus 20:12*.
We quickly disappear—*Job 14:1,2*.
Wicked will never live long—*Ecclesiastes 8:13*.

AGREEABLE

Agree wholeheartedly—*Philippians 2:2*.
Brothers live together in harmony—*Psalm 133:1*.
Can two walk together without agreeing?—*Amos 3:3*.
Live in harmony and peace—*Psalm 133:1*.
Stop arguing among yourselves—*1 Corinthians 1:10*.

ALCOHOL

Be filled with Spirit, not drunk on wine—*Ephesians 5:18*.
Do not cause brother to stumble—*Romans 14:21*.
Helps the dying—*Proverbs 31:6*.
Jesus turned water to wine—*John 2:1-11*.
Leads to brawls—*Proverbs 20:1*.
Leads to incapacitation—*Isaiah 28:1,7*.
Medicinal purposes—*1 Timothy 5:23*.
New wine, old wineskins—*Matthew 9:17; Mark 2:22*.
Robs people of clear thinking—*Hosea 4:11*.

ALMS (GOOD DEEDS)

Do good and share with others—*Hebrews 13:16*.
Do privately—*Matthew 6:1*.
Give to the poor—*Matthew 19:21; Luke 11:41; 12:33*.
Give to those who ask—*Matthew 5:42*.
Help the poor—*Deuteronomy 15:7; Galatians 2:10*.
Share food with the hungry—*Isaiah 58:7,10*.
Share money generously—*Romans 12:8*.
Use money for good—*1 Timothy 6:17,18*.

Ambition, Warnings Regarding

Better to be a servant—*Luke 22:26,27*.

Beware of devil's temptations—*Matthew 4:3-11*.

Do not be concerned about who is greatest—*Luke 9:46-48*.

Exalted will be humbled—*Matthew 23:12*.

Gain the world, lose your soul—*Matthew 16:26*.

Watch out for jealousy—*James 4:2*.

Watch out for religious hypocrisy—*Mark 12:38-40*.

Wealth by unjust means wrong—*Habakkuk 2:9*.

Wealth can be treacherous—*Habakkuk 2:5*.

Amusement

Can end in sorrow—*Proverbs 14:13*.

Can lead to evil—*Job 1:4,5*.

Can lead to poverty—*Proverbs 21:17*.

Angels

A hundred million—*Daniel 7:10*.

Created prior to creation of earth—*Job 38:7*.

God commanded and the angels were created—*Psalm 148:2,5*.

Good angels are "elect" angels—*1 Timothy 5:21*.

Innumerable—*Hebrews 12:22*.

Interested in plan of redemption—*1 Peter 1:12*.

Michael is archangel—*Jude 9*.

Seraphim proclaim God's holiness—*Isaiah 6:1-3*.

World will not be ruled by angels—*Hebrews 2:5*.

Nature of

Can take on appearance of humans—*Hebrews 13:2*.

Distinct from humans—*Psalm 8:4,5.*

Have emotions—*Luke 2:13.*

Have intellect—*1 Peter 1:12.*

Have wills—*Jude 6.*

Invisible to our eyes—*2 Kings 6:17.*

Ministering spirits—*Hebrews 2:14.*

No marriage—*Matthew 22:30.*

Very powerful—*Psalm 103:20.*

Ranks of

Archangel—*Jude 9.*

Cherubim—*Genesis 3:22-24.*

Chief princes—*Daniel 10:13.*

Different ranks—*Ephesians 3:10; Colossians 1:16.*

Guardian angels—*Matthew 18:10.*

Ruling angels—*Ephesians 3:10.*

Seraphim—*Isaiah 6:1-3.*

ANGER

Avoid angry people—*Proverbs 22:24,25.*

Be patient—*Proverbs 16:32.*

Be slow to anger—*James 1:19.*

Causes quarrels—*Proverbs 30:33.*

Characteristic of fools—*Ecclesiastes 7:9.*

Do not sin with anger—*Ephesians 4:26.*

Fool is quick-tempered—*Proverbs 12:16.*

Gentle answer turns away wrath—*Proverbs 15:1.*

Get rid of anger—*Ephesians 4:31; Colossians 3:8.*

Hothead starts fights—*Proverbs 15:18; 29:22.*

Restrain anger—*Proverbs 19:11.*

Short-tempered people do foolish things—*Proverbs 14:17*.
Those who control anger are wise—*Proverbs 14:29*.

ANIMALS

Adam named—*Genesis 2:19,20*.
Animals are God's—*Psalm 50:10*.
Clean and unclean—*Leviticus 20:25*.
Eating animals for food—*Genesis 9:3*.
God created animals—*Genesis 1:24*.
God feeds animals—*Psalm 147:9; Matthew 6:26*.
God provides for animals—*Genesis 1:30*.
Saved during flood—*Genesis 6:19,20*.
Wolf and lamb together—*Isaiah 11:6*.

ANOINTING

Anointing of Holy Spirit—*1 John 2:20*.
God anoints with oil of joy—*Psalm 45:7*.
Healing and anointing with oil—*Mark 6:13; James 5:14*.
Jesus was anointed with burial spices—*Mark 16:1*.
Jesus was anointed with perfume—*Matthew 26:12*.

ANTICHRIST

Denies Christ—*1 John 2:22; 2 John 7*.
Denies incarnation—*1 John 4:3; 2 John 7*.
Destiny is Lake of Fire—*Revelation 19:20*.
Dominion of, during Tribulation Period—*Revelation 13*.
Is coming—*1 John 2:18*.
Man of lawlessness—*2 Thessalonians 2:1-10*.
Spirit of Antichrist—*1 John 4:3*.

ANXIETY

Cast all anxiety on God—*1 Peter 5:7*.

Do not worry about anything—*Philippians 4:6,7*.
Do not worry about tomorrow—*Matthew 6:31-33*.
God will supply all needs—*Philippians 4:19*.
Hope in God as a cure—*Psalm 43:5*.

APATHY

Hard hearts—*Ezekiel 2:4; Mark 6:52; Ephesians 4:18*.
No concern about right and wrong—*Ephesians 4:19*.
No concern for God or man, a parable—*Luke 18:1-5*.
Refusal to hear or see—*Ezekiel 12:2*.

APOLOGETICS

Apollos contended for the faith—*Acts 18:24-28*.
Be ready with answer—*1 Peter 3:15*.
Contend for the faith—*Jude 3*.

APOSTASY

Do not be carried away by error—*2 Peter 3:17*.
Do not turn from God—*Hebrews 3:12*.
End-times rebellion—*2 Thessalonians 2:3*.
Idolatrous priests—*Zephaniah 1:4*.
Many turn from truth in last days—*1 Timothy 4:1*.
Many will turn from Christ—*Matthew 24:10,11*.
People will reject truth—*2 Timothy 4:4*.
People will turn from right teaching—*2 Timothy 4:3*.

APOSTLES

Names of 12 apostles—*Matthew 10:2-4*.
Performed miraculous signs—*Acts 2:43; 5:12*.
Powerful witnesses—*Acts 4:33*.
Proof of apostleship—*2 Corinthians 12:12*.
Sent out to preach—*Mark 3:14*.

False

False apostles deceive—*2 Corinthians 11:13*.

False apostles lie—*Revelation 2:2*.

False prophets—*Matthew 7:15; 24:11; Mark 13:22*.

False teachers—*Matthew 5:19; 15:9; 1 Timothy 1:7; 4:2*.

APPETITE

Feed hungry—*Matthew 25:34-46*.

Feed hungry enemies—*Proverbs 25:21,22*.

God fills the hungry with good things—*Psalm 107:9*.

Jesus fasted 40 days—*Matthew 4:2; Luke 4:2*.

Lazy person goes hungry—*Proverbs 19:15*.

Overly concerned for food—*Luke 12:22,29*.

APPRECIATION

Appreciate church leaders—*1 Thessalonians 5:12,13*.

Honest answers appreciated—*Proverbs 24:26*.

No appreciation shown—*Psalm 78:9-21*.

APPREHENSION

Anxious thoughts, God is aware of—*Psalm 139:23*.

Do not worry—*Exodus 14:14*.

Fear not, God is with you—*Psalm 23:4*.

God has not given us spirit of fear—*2 Timothy 1:7*.

Let not your heart be troubled—*John 14:27*.

Whom shall I fear?—*Psalm 27:1*.

ARGUMENT

Contentious wife—*Proverbs 25:24*.

Fools insist on quarreling—*Proverbs 20:3*.

Quarreling, outbursts of anger—*2 Corinthians 12:20*.

Stay away from arguing—*Philippians 2:14*.

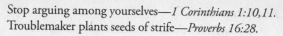

Stop arguing among yourselves—*1 Corinthians 1:10,11*.

Troublemaker plants seeds of strife—*Proverbs 16:28*.

ARK, NOAH'S

Kept Noah's family and animals safe—*Genesis 6:13,14,18-20*.

Noah acted in faith in building—*Hebrews 11:7*.

Noah saved because of righteousness—*Genesis 7:1*.

Rested on Ararat—*Genesis 8:4*.

ARK OF THE COVENANT

Behind inner curtain, Most Holy Place—*Exodus 26:33*.

Captured—*1 Samuel 4:11-22*.

Contained stone tablets—*Exodus 25:16,21; 40:20*.

Description of contents—*Hebrews 9:4*.

Dimensions of—*Exodus 25:10; 37:1*.

ARMAGEDDON

Christ returns at height of—*Revelation 19:11-21*.

Devastating to humanity—*Matthew 24:22*.

Place of final battle—*Revelation 16:14,16*.

ARMOR, SPIRITUAL

Clothe yourselves with armor of light—*Romans 13:12,13*.

Put on all of God's armor—*Ephesians 6:11-18*.

Put on armor of faith, love, and hope—*1 Thessalonians 5:8*.

ARROGANCE

Boastful tongue—*Psalm 12:3,4*.

Do not speak with arrogance—*1 Samuel 2:3*.

God hates arrogance—*Proverbs 8:13*.

God will crush arrogance of the proud—*Isaiah 13:11*.

Ashamed

Adam and Eve naked, felt no shame—*Genesis 2:25.*

After sin, Adam and Eve felt shame—*Genesis 3:7,10.*

Fool put to shame—*Proverbs 3:35.*

Never be ashamed to tell others about Christ—
2 Timothy 1:8.

Prayer to avoid shame—*Psalm 31:1.*

Sin leads to shame and disgrace—*Genesis 3:7.*

Assurance of Salvation

Assurance based on Scripture—*1 John 5:10-13.*

Assurance from Christ—*John 5:24.*

God can keep us from falling—*Jude 1:24.*

Holy Spirit testifies we are God's children—*Romans 8:16.*

Jesus intercedes for us—*Hebrews 7:25.*

Nothing can separate us from God—*Romans 8:38,39.*

Secure in Father's hand—*John 10:29.*

We are sealed by Holy Spirit—*Ephesians 4:30.*

Astrology

Astrologers cannot interpret dreams—*Daniel 4:7.*

Astrologers cannot save you—*Isaiah 47:13,14.*

Do not try to read future in stars—*Jeremiah 10:2.*

Astronomy

God created stars—*Isaiah 40:26; Amos 5:8.*

God made heavens beautiful—*Job 26:13; Psalm 136:5.*

God provides light by sun and moon—*Jeremiah 31:35.*

Heavens declare God's glory—*Psalm 19:1.*

Stars cannot be counted—*Jeremiah 33:22.*

ATHEISM

Ask the animals, they will tell you—*Job 12:7-9.*

Fool says there is no God—*Psalm 14:1; 53:1.*

God's existence evident in creation—*Romans 1:20.*

God's truth in human heart proves His existence—
Romans 1:18,19.

ATHLETICS

Archery—*Genesis 21:20.*

Boxing—*1 Corinthians 9:26.*

Do not lose race—*Philippians 2:16.*

Fight a good fight—*2 Timothy 4:7.*

In race, only one gets prize—*1 Corinthians 9:24.*

Run with endurance—*Hebrews 12:1.*

ATONEMENT

Day of

No work to be done—*Numbers 29:7.*

Once a year—*Exodus 30:10; Hebrews 9:7.*

Extent of

Christ is Savior of all—*1 Timothy 4:10.*

Christ made atonement for all—*1 John 2:2.*

Christ made salvation provision for whole world—
2 Corinthians 5:19.

Christ paid price for all men—*1 Timothy 2:5,6.*

Made by Jesus

Died for our sins—*1 Peter 3:18.*

Once and for all—*Hebrews 7:27; 10:12.*

Our Passover Lamb—*1 Corinthians 5:7.*

Purchased church with blood—*Acts 20:28.*

Purchased our freedom—*Revelation 5:9*.
Ransomed many—*Matthew 20:28; 1 Timothy 2:6*.
Secured our salvation forever—*Hebrews 9:12*.
Took away our sins—*Hebrews 9:28*.

ATTITUDE

Attitude toward suffering—*1 Peter 4:12-16*.
Bad attitude—*Genesis 4:3-7; Deuteronomy 20:8*.
Be gentle—*Philippians 4:5*.
Be humble—*Luke 7:6,7*.
Be kind—*Ephesians 4:32*.
Be merciful—*Luke 6:36*.
Disregard people's faults—*Proverbs 17:9*.
Do everything with love—*1 Corinthians 16:14*.
Fix thoughts on what is true, honorable, right—
    Philippians 4:8.
Happy heart—*Proverbs 15:13*.
Let heaven fill thoughts—*Colossians 3:1,2*.

ATTORNEY

Come to terms quickly with enemy—*Matthew 5:25*.
Do not be in hurry to go to court—*Proverbs 25:8*.
Why file lawsuit against Christians?—*1 Corinthians 6:1*.

AUTHORITY

Accept all authority—*1 Peter 2:13*.
Authority of disciples over demons—*Matthew 10:1*.
Christ in authority over all—*Matthew 11:27*.
Father gave Jesus authority—*John 3:35*.
God sovereign above all authority—*Ephesians 1:20-22*.
Wife should accept authority of husband—*1 Peter 3:1*.

BAAL

Altars to—*2 Chronicles 33:3*.

Prophets killed—*1 Kings 18:40*.

Seven thousand in Israel never bowed to—*1 Kings 19:18*.

Worship of—*2 Chronicles 28:2*.

BACKSLIDING

God's Word helps you not slip—*Psalm 37:31*.

Persevere in commitment—*2 Timothy 2:12,13*.

Put hand to plow, do not look back—*Luke 9:62*.

Watch out for false gospels—*Galatians 1:6*.

Watch out for love of money—*1 Timothy 6:10*.

Watch yourself carefully—*Deuteronomy 4:9*.

BAD EXAMPLE

Concubines led Solomon astray—*1 Kings 11:3,4*.

Do not be influenced by bad example—*3 John 11*.

Do not be stumbling block—*1 Corinthians 8:9,13*.

Eve influenced Adam—*Genesis 3:6*.

Jezebel influenced Ahab—*1 Kings 21:25*.

Judaizers influenced Galatians—*Galatians 3:1*.

BAPTISM

Baptism in name of Father, Son, Spirit—*Matthew 28:19*.

Baptized into Christ—*Galatians 3:27,28*.

Believe and be baptized—*Mark 16:16*.

Buried with Christ in baptism—*Romans 6:4*.

Repent and be baptized—*Acts 2:38*.

BEAUTY

Beauty does not last—*Proverbs 31:30.*
Do not be concerned about outward beauty—*1 Peter 3:3.*
Unfading beauty of a gentle spirit—*1 Peter 3:4.*

BEHAVIOR

Behave well among Gentiles—*1 Peter 2:12.*
Blameless—*Psalm 15:2.*
Clean, innocent—*Romans 16:19; Philippians 2:15.*
Clear conscience—*2 Corinthians 1:12.*
Exemplary behavior—*Philippians 1:9,10; 1 Timothy 3:2.*
Get rid of malicious behavior—*Ephesians 4:31.*
Holy behavior—*1 Peter 1:15.*

BELIEVERS

Belong to the Lamb—*Revelation 13:8.*
Holy Spirit fills—*Ephesians 5:18.*
Holy Spirit indwells—*1 Corinthians 6:19.*
Holy Spirit produces fruit in—*Galatians 5:22,23.*
Holy Spirit seals for day of redemption—*Ephesians 4:30.*
Judged by Christ—*1 Corinthians 3:10-15.*
Satan accuses and slanders—*Job 1:9-11.*
Satan plants doubt in minds of—*Genesis 3:1-5.*
Satan tempts to immorality—*1 Corinthians 7:5.*
Will be resurrected—*Revelation 20:4-6.*
Will never perish—*John 10:28.*

BEREAVEMENT AND LOSS

Even if parents forsake you, God will not—*Psalm 27:10.*
God's Word comforts us—*Psalm 119:50.*
God's Word sustains us—*Psalm 119:92.*
Knowing Jesus makes up for our loss—*Philippians 3:8.*

BETHLEHEM

Children killed in—*Matthew 2:16*.
Jesus born in—*Micah 5:2; Matthew 2:1*.

BETRAYAL

Best friends may betray—*Psalm 41:9*.
Family members may betray—*Matthew 10:21*.
Joseph betrayed by brothers—*Genesis 37:21-28; 50:20*.
Judas Iscariot's betrayal—*Matthew 26:14-16*.
Son of Man will be betrayed—*Matthew 20:18*.

BIBLE

Feeds the soul—*Deuteronomy 8:3; Psalm 119:103*.
Gives hope—*Romans 15:4*.
Gives us light—*Psalm 19:8; 119:105,130; Proverbs 6:23*.
Inspired by God—*2 Timothy 3:16; 2 Peter 1:21*.
Powerful influence—*Ephesians 6:17; Hebrews 4:12*.
Purifies us—*Psalm 119:9; John 17:17; Ephesians 5:25,26*.
Teaches us—*Deuteronomy 4:10; 2 Chronicles 17:9*.
Tells us about eternal life—*1 John 5:13*.
Trustworthy—*Psalm 111:7*.
We should not be ignorant of—*Matthew 22:29*.

BIRTH

Day of death better than day of birth—*Ecclesiastes 7:1*.
God controls in womb—*Psalm 139:15,16; Jeremiah 1:5*.
Intense pain and suffering—*Genesis 3:16*.
Jeremiah set apart before birth—*Jeremiah 1:5*.
Paul called before birth—*Galatians 1:15*.
Virgin will give birth, Messiah—*Isaiah 7:14*.
We are sinful from moment of birth—*Psalm 51:5*.

BIRTHDAY

Herod's birthday—*Matthew 14:6.*
Pharaoh's birthday—*Genesis 40:20.*

BITTERNESS

Bitterness of spirit—*Deuteronomy 32:32.*
Do not harbor bitter envy—*James 3:14.*
Do not let bitter root grow—*Hebrews 12:15.*
Get rid of all bitterness—*Ephesians 4:31.*

BLAME

Adam and Eve passed the buck—*Genesis 3:12,13.*
Be without blame at Second Coming—*1 Thessalonians 5:23.*
Job did not blame God—*Job 1:22.*
Joseph's brothers realize blame—*Genesis 42:21,22.*

BLASPHEMY

Antichrist blasphemes—*2 Thessalonians 2:4.*
Blasphemy against Spirit not forgiven—*Matthew 12:31,32.*
Do not misuse name of Lord—*Exodus 20:7.*
Do not treat God's holy name as common—*Leviticus 22:32.*
Do not use God's name to swear a falsehood—*Leviticus 19:12.*

BLESSING

Contingent on Obedience

Be careful to obey—*Exodus 19:5; 23:22.*
Keep God's laws—*Leviticus 26:3; 1 Kings 2:3.*
Obey God's regulations—*Deuteronomy 7:12.*

Spiritual

God arms me with strength—*Psalm 18:32; 144:1.*
God is the strength of my heart—*Psalm 73:26.*
God renews my strength—*Psalm 23:3; 29:11.*
God will uphold you—*Isaiah 41:10.*
God's hand supports me—*Psalm 18:35; 63:8.*
Though we stumble, we will not fall—*Psalm 37:24.*
We will run and not grow weary—*Isaiah 40:31.*

Temporal

All will go well —*Deuteronomy 12:28.*
Avoid diseases—*Exodus 15:26.*
Bear many children—*Deuteronomy 7:13.*
Enjoy long life—*Deuteronomy 4:40; 5:33.*
Food and water provided—*Exodus 23:25; Psalm 111:5.*
Never lack any good thing—*Psalm 34:10.*
No need to worry about everyday life—*Luke 12:22.*
Plenty of provisions—*2 Corinthians 9:8.*
Prosper in everything—*Deuteronomy 28:8.*
Riches, wealth, honor—*2 Chronicles 1:12.*

BLINDNESS

Angels blinded men of Sodom—*Genesis 19:11.*
Messiah helps the blind see—*Matthew 11:5.*
Saul was blinded—*Acts 9:8,9.*
Two blind men healed by Jesus—*Matthew 9:27-30.*

Spiritual

Blind guides—*Matthew 15:14; 23:16,26.*
Fools say there is no God—*Psalm 14:1.*
Minds full of darkness—*Ephesians 4:18.*

Open my eyes—*Psalm 119:18*.
Satan blinds minds—*2 Corinthians 4:4*.
Unbelievers blind to truth—*1 Corinthians 2:14,15*.

Blood

Blood smeared on doorposts—*Exodus 12:7,13*.
Crime leads to bloodshed—*Genesis 9:6*.
Do not eat blood—*Genesis 9:4; Leviticus 17:10,11,14*.
Moon will become red as blood—*Joel 2:31;
    Acts 2:20*.
Nile River turned to blood—*Exodus 7:17-20*.

Of Christ

Cleanses us from sin—*1 John 1:7*.
Freed us from sin—*Revelation 1:5*.
Made us right with God—*Romans 5:9*.
Purchased church—*Acts 20:28*.
Purchased our freedom—*Colossians 1:14,20*.
Ransomed people from every tribe—*Revelation 5:9*.

Boasting

Better to be lowly in spirit—*Proverbs 16:19*.
Boast in God—*Psalm 44:8*.
Boast in the cross—*Galatians 6:14*.
Boast in the Lord—*Psalm 34:2; 1 Corinthians 1:31*.
Boasting is evil—*James 4:16*.
Do not be conceited—*Romans 12:16*.
Do not brag—*James 3:13*.
God humbles the proud—*Isaiah 13:11; Daniel 4:37*.
Let not wise man boast—*Jeremiah 9:23*.
Pride goes before destruction—*Proverbs 16:18; 18:12*.

Body of Christ

Build up body of Christ—*Ephesians 4:11-13*.
Christ is head of church—*Ephesians 5:23*.
Equality in body of Christ—*Galatians 3:26-28*.

Boldness of Believers

Be full of courage—*1 John 2:28*.
Come boldly to throne of grace—*Hebrews 4:16*.
Come fearlessly into God's presence—*Ephesians 3:12*.

Bondage

Believers are delivered from—*Romans 6:18,22*.
Bondage to devil—*1 Timothy 3:7*.
Bondage to sin—*Acts 8:23; Romans 6:16*.
Enslavement to sinful desires—*1 Corinthians 3:3*.

Book of Life

Christians' names in—*Philippians 4:3*.
God will never erase believers' names—*Revelation 3:5*.
Rejoice, names registered in heaven—*Luke 10:20*.

Born Again

Born again to living hope—*1 Peter 1:3*.
New birth—*1 Peter 1:23*.
You must be born again—*John 3:5-7*.

Bribery

Corrupts the heart—*Ecclesiastes 7:7*.
Never accept—*Exodus 23:8; Deuteronomy 16:19*.
Those who hate bribes will live—*Proverbs 15:27*.

BRIDE

Beauty of bride—*Song of Solomon 4.*
Bride of Christ—*Revelation 19:7; 21:2.*
Good wife, favor from the Lord—*Proverbs 18:22.*
Kindness of wife—*Proverbs 31:26.*
Share your love only with wife—*Proverbs 5:15,18.*

BROTHER

Build up brothers—*Luke 22:32.*
Do not cause brother to stumble—*Romans 14:21.*
Feed and give water to brothers—*Matthew 25:37-40.*
Friend closer than brother—*Proverbs 18:24.*
Help brothers in need—*1 John 3:16-18.*
If brother sins, show him fault—*Matthew 18:15-17.*
Love your Christian brothers—*1 Peter 2:17.*
Maintain brotherly kindness—*2 Peter 1:5-7.*
Never cheat Christian brother—*1 Thessalonians 4:6.*
Reconcile with brother—*Matthew 5:23,24.*
Restore fallen brothers—*Galatians 6:1.*

BURIAL

Burial spices—*Mark 16:1.*
Bury body same day—*Deuteronomy 21:23.*
Funeral procession—*Luke 7:12.*

BUSINESS ETHICS

Be diligent—*Proverbs 10:4; 13:4; 22:29; 2 Peter 3:14.*
Be fair—*Leviticus 19:36; Deuteronomy 25:13.*
Be faithful—*Genesis 39:6,8; 2 Kings 12:15; Daniel 6:4.*
Be honest—*Leviticus 19:35,36; Proverbs 11:1.*
Be industrious—*Proverbs 6:6-8; 10:5; 12:11; 13:11.*

Maintain integrity—*Psalm 41:12; Proverbs 11:3; 19:1.*
No extortion—*Isaiah 10:12; Ezekiel 22:12; Amos 5:11.*
No slothfulness—*Proverbs 18:9; 24:30,31.*
No unjust gain—*Proverbs 16:8; 21:6; Jeremiah 17:11.*
Pay prompt wages—*Deuteronomy 24:15.*

CALAMITY

Day of disaster—*Psalm 18:18.*
Guarding the mouth averts—*Proverbs 21:23.*
Will overtake the wicked—*Psalm 34:21.*

CALL TO SERVICE

Barnabas and Saul called—*Acts 13:2.*
Disciples invited—*Matthew 9:9; Mark 1:16,17.*
Isaiah called—*Isaiah 6:8.*
Jeremiah set apart before birth—*Jeremiah 1:5.*
Paul chosen to be apostle—*Romans 1:1.*

CANON OF SCRIPTURE

Do not change God's words—*Revelation 22:18-20.*
Luke's Gospel recognized as Scripture—*1 Timothy 5:18.*
Old Testament recognized as Scripture—*Matthew 5:17.*
Paul's writings recognized as Scripture—*2 Peter 3:16.*

CAPITAL PUNISHMENT

Deterrent to crime—*Deuteronomy 17:12.*
For adultery—*John 8:3-11.*
For idolatry—*Exodus 22:20.*
For kidnapping—*Exodus 21:16.*
For mediums, psychics, sorcerers—*Exodus 22:18.*
For murder—*Genesis 9:6; Leviticus 24:17.*
Instituted by God—*Genesis 9:6.*

CAPTIVITY (FIGURATIVE)

Captive to desires—*2 Timothy 3:2,6.*
Captive to sin—*Romans 7:23.*
Captive to the devil—*2 Timothy 2:26.*

Overcoming captivity to rebellious ideas—
2 Corinthians 10:5.

CARE, WORLDLY

Be free from concerns of life—*1 Corinthians 7:32.*
Busy rushing ends in nothing—*Psalm 39:6.*
Do not be tied up in affairs of life—*2 Timothy 2:4.*
Do not worry about anything—*Matthew 6:25.* ✔

CARNALITY

Carousing—*2 Peter 2:13-16.*
Cravings of sin, lust of eyes, boasting—*1 John 2:16.*
Do not be attached to world—*1 Corinthians 7:29-31.*
Do not be conformed to world—*Romans 12:2.*
Fleshly living—*1 Corinthians 3:3.*
Indulging in sinful nature—*Romans 8:5; Galatians 5:13.*
Loving all the wrong things—*2 Timothy 3:2-7.*

CAUTION

Be careful how you live—*Ephesians 5:15.*
Be careful lest you fall—*1 Corinthians 10:12.*
Be careful to love Lord—*Joshua 23:11.*
Be careful to obey God—*Exodus 19:5; 23:22.*
Caution in friendship—*Proverbs 12:26.*
Watch yourself carefully—*Deuteronomy 4:9.*

CELIBACY

Better not to marry—*Matthew 19:10.*
Be free from concerns of life—*1 Corinthians 7:32.*
Celibate life is good—*1 Corinthians 7:1.*
Get along without marrying—*1 Corinthians 7:7.*
Remain just as you are—*1 Corinthians 7:26,27.*

CHARACTER

Firmness of

Endure to the end—*Matthew 10:22.*
Hold tightly to hope—*Hebrews 10:23.*
Stand firm—*2 Thessalonians 2:15.*

Of Saints

Blameless—*Psalm 15:2.*
Clean, innocent—*Romans 16:19; Philippians 2:15.*
Clear conscience—*2 Corinthians 1:12.*
Devout—*Luke 2:25; Acts 10:2.*
Generous—*Isaiah 32:8; 2 Corinthians 9:13.*
Gentle and lowly—*Matthew 5:5.*
Holy—*Deuteronomy 7:6.*
Honest—*John 1:47; 2 Corinthians 6:4,8.*
Live by faith—*Habakkuk 2:4.*
Love each other—*1 Thessalonians 4:9.*
Merciful—*Matthew 5:7; Colossians 3:12.*
Obedient to God—*Luke 1:6.*

Of Wicked

Betray friends—*2 Timothy 3:2-4.*
Corrupt—*Deuteronomy 32:5; Romans 1:29.*
Deny God—*Psalm 14:1; Acts 7:51; Romans 3:11.*
Depraved minds—*2 Timothy 3:8.*
Dishonest—*Psalm 62:4; Micah 6:11.*
Disobedient—*Nehemiah 9:26.*
Evil desires—*Psalm 10:2-4; Isaiah 59:7.*
Foolish—*Titus 3:3.*
Foul talk—*Romans 3:13.*

Hypocritical—*Isaiah 29:13.*

Love themselves and money—*2 Timothy 3:2.*

Lustful—*Ephesians 4:22.*

Plot evil—*Isaiah 59:4.*

Proud—*Psalm 5:4,5; 10:4.*

Unconcerned about right and wrong—*Ephesians 4:19.*

CHARISMATIC ISSUES

God pours out Spirit on all people—*Ezekiel 39:29.*

Instructions about laying on of hands—*Hebrews 6:1,2.*

Lay hands and heal—*Mark 16:18.*

Speaking in tongues—*Acts 2:7-11; 10:46; 19:6.*

CHARITABLE ATTITUDE

Accept Christians weak in faith—*Romans 14:1.*

Be clothed with love—*Colossians 3:14.*

Be compassionate—*Luke 6:36.*

Be filled with love—*1 Timothy 1:5.*

Be kind—*Ephesians 4:32.*

Disregard people's faults—*Proverbs 17:9.*

Make allowance for people's faults—*Colossians 3:13.*

CHEATING

Dishonesty an abomination to God—*Proverbs 20:23.*

Do not cheat anyone—*Leviticus 19:13.*

Do not cheat employees of wages—*Jeremiah 22:13.*

Do not cheat Lord—*Malachi 3:8,9.*

Do not get rich by extortion—*Psalm 62:10.*

Do not use dishonest standards—*Leviticus 19:35.*

Lord hates cheating—*Proverbs 11:1.*

Never cheat Christian brother—*1 Thessalonians 4:6.*

CHILDREN

Do not despise children—*Matthew 18:10*.
Gift from God—*Psalm 127:3*.
Jesus' attitude toward children—*Luke 18:16*.
Parents are the pride of their children—*Proverbs 17:6*.
To such belong kingdom of God—*Matthew 19:14*.

Commandments to Children

Honor father and mother—*Exodus 20:12*.
Listen to what parents teach—*Proverbs 1:8; 6:20; 23:22*.
Obey parents—*Ephesians 6:1; Colossians 3:20*.
Respect parents—*Leviticus 19:3*.

Discipline of

Discipline children—*Proverbs 13:24; 19:18; 29:17*.
Discipline drives away foolishness—*Proverbs 22:15*.
Discipline produces wisdom—*Proverbs 29:15*.

Good

Are pleasing to the Lord—*Colossians 3:20*.
Bring joy to father—*Proverbs 23:24*.
Will live long—*Ephesians 6:2,3*.

Wicked

Despise and defy parents—*Deuteronomy 27:16*.
Disobedient—*Romans 1:30; 2 Timothy 3:2*.
Foolish—*Proverbs 10:1; 15:5,20; 17:25*.
Mistreat parents—*Exodus 21:15; Proverbs 19:26*.
Rebel—*Deuteronomy 21:18; Proverbs 17:21; Mark 13:12*.
Rob parents—*Proverbs 28:24*.
Shameful—*Proverbs 17:2*.

CHOICE

Choose good, not evil—*Amos 5:15*.

Choose life—*Deuteronomy 30:19*.

Choose Lord—*Genesis 28:21; Psalm 16:2; 140:6*.

Choose way of truth—*Psalm 119:30*.

Choose whom you will follow—*Joshua 24:15*.

Choosing right over wrong—*1 Kings 3:9*.

CHRISTMAS

Child is born to us—*Isaiah 9:6; Luke 1:35*.

Jesus born in Bethlehem—*Micah 5:2; Matthew 2:4,5*.

Jesus born of a woman—*Genesis 3:15; Galatians 4:4*.

Jesus born of virgin—*Isaiah 7:14; Matthew 1:23*.

CHURCH

Body of Christ—*Colossians 1:18*.

Bride of Christ—*Revelation 21:2*.

God's household—*1 Timothy 3:14,15*.

God's temple—*1 Corinthians 3:16*.

Jesus builds church—*Matthew 16:18*.

One body, many members—*Romans 12:4,5*.

Christ in Authority over

Christ is cornerstone—*Ephesians 2:20; 1 Peter 2:7*.

Christ is the foundation—*1 Corinthians 3:11*.

Christ is the head—*Colossians 1:18; 2:19*.

Discipline in

After discipline, restoration—*2 Corinthians 2:6-8*.

Correct when necessary—*Titus 2:15*.

Excommunication—*2 Thessalonians 3:14*.

Jesus commends church for discipline—*Revelation 2:2*.

Proper protocol for discipline—*Matthew 18:15-17*.
Rebuke when necessary—*Titus 1:13*.
Restore one who has fallen—*Galatians 6:1*.
Seek to save erring sinner—*James 5:19,20*.

Government of

Appointment of deacons—*Acts 6:1-6*.
Appointment of elders—*Acts 14:23; Titus 1:5*.
Instructions to elders—*Acts 20:17,28; 1 Peter 5:1-4*.
Qualifications for elders and deacons—*1 Timothy 3:1-13; Titus 1:6-9*.

Mission of

Be Christ's witnesses—*Luke 24:45-49; Acts 1:7,8*.
Build up body of Christ—*Ephesians 4:11-13*.
Do good to all people—*Galatians 6:10; Titus 3:14*.
Exercise spiritual gifts—*Romans 12:6-8*.
Financially support God's work—*1 Corinthians 16:1-3*.
Help brothers in need—*1 John 3:16-18*.
Make disciples—*Matthew 28:19,20*.
Offer hospitality to each other—*1 Peter 4:9-11*.
Preach the Word—*Mark 16:15,16; 1 Timothy 4:6,13*.
Take care of orphans and widows—*1 Timothy 5:3,4,16*.
Take care of the sick—*James 5:14,15*.

Unity of

One flock with one shepherd—*John 10:16*.
Peace between Jews and Gentiles—*Ephesians 2:14,21*.
We are one body—*1 Corinthians 10:17; 12:12*.

CITIZENS

Duties of

Accept all authority—*1 Peter 2:13*.

Fear the Lord and the king—*Proverbs 24:21*.

Obey the government—*Romans 13:1,5; Titus 3:1*.

Pray for kings and others in authority—*1 Timothy 2:1,2*.

Rights of

Citizenship in heaven—*Philippians 3:20*.

Rights of citizens—*Nehemiah 5:4-13*.

Violation of Roman citizenship—*Acts 16:37; 22:25*.

CLEANLINESS

Clean hands—*Job 17:9*.

Cleansing ceremony—*Leviticus 14:8,9*.

Hearts sprinkled clean—*Hebrews 10:22*.

Purification, shave and wash—*Numbers 8:7*.

Purify and change clothes—*Genesis 35:2*.

Wash face—*Matthew 6:17*.

CLERGY

God gives servants to the church—*Ephesians 4:11*.

Pray over the sick—*James 5:14,15*.

Preach the Word—*Mark 16:15; 1 Timothy 4:6,13*.

Sent out to preach—*Mark 3:14*.

CLOUD, PILLAR OF

Cloud of glory—*Isaiah 6:1-5*.

Cloud upon Mount Sinai—*Exodus 16:10; 19:16; 24:16*.

Lord appeared in pillar of cloud—*Deuteronomy 31:15*.

Lord guided Israelites by pillar—*Exodus 13:21,22*.

COLOR

Blue cloth—*Exodus 28:28,31; Numbers 4:7.*
Blue, purple, scarlet material—*Exodus 26:1.*
Clothed in white—*Revelation 4:4; 7:9.*
Purple cloth—*Numbers 4:13.*
Red as crimson, white as wool—*Isaiah 1:18.*
Scarlet cloth—*Leviticus 14:4,49,51; Numbers 4:8.*
White robe—*Revelation 6:11.*

COMFORT

Christ gives us rest—*Matthew 11:28-30.*
Comforter is with you—*John 14:16-18.*
Fear not, God is with you—*Psalm 23:4.*
God consoles us—*2 Thessalonians 2:16,17.*
God of all comfort is with you—*2 Corinthians 1:3,4.*
Scripture comforts us—*Romans 15:4.*
Those who mourn will be comforted—*Matthew 5:4.*

COMMITMENT

Count the cost—*Matthew 8:19,20.*
Do not look back—*Luke 9:62.*
Keep vow to God—*Psalm 65:1; Ecclesiastes 5:4,5.*
Living sacrifice—*Romans 12:1.*
Love shows commitment—*1 John 2:9-11.*
Persevere in commitment—*2 Timothy 2:12,13.*
Totally committed—*Joshua 24:14; Titus 2:13,14.*

COMMUNION

Of Saints

Brothers living together in harmony—*Psalm 133:1.*
Build each other up—*Luke 22:32; 1 Thessalonians 5:11.*

Encourage each other—*1 Thessalonians 4:18.*
Good fellowship—*Psalm 55:13,14.*
Maintain unity—*John 17:21.*
Pray for each other—*James 5:16.*

With God

Comforter never leaves us—*John 14:16.*
Father and Jesus live with us—*John 14:23.*
Lord guides us—*Psalm 16:7.*
Our fellowship is with Father and Son—*1 John 1:3.*

COMPANIONSHIP

Can two walk together without agreeing?—*Amos 3:3.*
Companionship among disciples—*Galatians 2:9.*
Companionship with Father and Jesus—*1 John 1:3.*
Companionship with righteous people—*Psalm 119:63.*
Two by two—*Luke 10:1.*

COMPANY, EVIL

Corrupts good character—*1 Corinthians 15:33.*
Do not carouse with drunkards—*Proverbs 23:20.*
Do not eat with stingy people—*Proverbs 23:6.*
Do not join crowd that intends evil—*Genesis 49:5,6.*
Do not participate in sins of others—*1 Timothy 5:22.*
Do not spend time with liars—*Psalm 26:4.*
Stay away from evil people—*Proverbs 1:10,15.*

COMPASSION

Be a Good Samaritan—*Luke 10:30-37.*
Be compassionate and humble—*1 Peter 3:8.*
Be compassionate to the poor—*Proverbs 19:17.*
Be compassionate to the weak—*Psalm 41:1.*

Be compassionate toward enemies—*Psalm 35:13*.

Be compassionate toward the afflicted—*Job 6:14*.

Do not just pretend to love others—*Romans 12:9,10*.

Love your neighbor as yourself—*Leviticus 19:18*.

COMPLAIN

Avoid complaining and arguing—*Philippians 2:14*.

Complaints against God—*Psalm 44:9-26*.

Complaints to God—*Psalm 142:2*.

Do not grumble—*John 6:43*.

God hears all complaints—*Numbers 14:27*.

Notable examples—*Genesis 4:13,14; Exodus 5:22,23*.

COMPROMISE

Believers cannot marry unbelievers—*1 Corinthians 7:16*.

Cannot serve two masters—*Matthew 6:24*.

Do compromise before litigation—*Proverbs 25:8-10*.

Do not assist in evil—*2 Chronicles 19:2*.

Do not blur good and evil—*Isaiah 5:20*.

Do not compromise in righteousness—*Psalm 119:3*.

Partial obedience unacceptable—*2 Kings 14:3,4*.

Seek to please God, not men—*1 Thessalonians 2:3,4*.

CONCEIT

Do not be impressed with your own wisdom—*Proverbs 3:7*.

Do not try to act important—*Romans 12:16*.

Hypocritical Pharisees—*Luke 18:11*.

Trusting oneself is foolish—*Proverbs 28:26*.

CONDEMNATION

Adam's sin brought—*Romans 5:18-21*.

Hypocrisy leads to—*Matthew 23:14*.
No condemnation in Christ—*Romans 8:1*.
Pride leads to—*1 Timothy 3:6*.
Unbelief leads to—*Mark 16:16; John 3:18*.
Unbelievers remain under—*John 3:18,36*.

CONDUCT, PROPER

Abstain from evil—*1 Thessalonians 5:22*.
Behave in manner worthy of gospel—*Philippians 1:27*.
Follow Golden Rule—*Matthew 7:12; Luke 6:31*.
Generous—*Romans 12:13*.
Live blamelessly—*Philippians 1:10; 2:15*.
Live soberly—*Titus 2:12*.
Put away sin—*Hebrews 12:1*.
Self-controlled—*1 Corinthians 9:27; 1 Timothy 3:2*.
Walk honestly—*1 Thessalonians 4:11,12*.
Walk worthy of the Lord—*Colossians 1:10*.

CONFESSION

Confess Jesus is Lord—*Romans 10:9*.
Confess sins, God forgives—*1 John 1:9*.
Confess sins to each other—*James 5:16*.
Personal sins confessed—*Joshua 7:20; 1 Samuel 15:24*.

CONFIDENCE

Boldness and confidence—*Ephesians 3:10-12*.
Can do all things through Christ—*Philippians 4:13*.
Do not cast away your confidence—*Hebrews 10:35*.
Fear not, God is with you—*Psalm 27:3,4*.
Lord is your confidence—*Proverbs 3:26*.

CONSCIENCE

Conscience can be seared—*1 Timothy 4:2*.

Conscience can become corrupted—*Titus 1:15*.

Conscience can confirm—*Romans 9:1*.

Evil conscience cleansed by Christ—*Hebrews 10:22*.

Keep a clear conscience—*2 Corinthians 1:12*.

Not bothered by evil—*Proverbs 30:20*.

Guilty

Be cleansed of guilty conscience—*Hebrews 10:22*.

David sought purification—*Psalm 51:7*.

Judas filled with remorse—*Matthew 27:3*.

CONSCIOUSNESS FOLLOWING DEATH

Absent from body, with Lord—*2 Corinthians 5:8*.

Depart and be with Christ—*Philippians 1:23*.

Rich man and Lazarus—*Luke 16:19-31*.

Souls under God's altar—*Revelation 6:9*.

Thief with Christ in paradise—*Luke 23:43*.

CONSECRATION

Be slaves of righteousness—*Romans 6:19*.

Give your bodies to God—*Romans 12:1*.

Give yourselves completely to God—*Romans 6:13*.

CONSISTENCY

Do not blur good and evil—*Isaiah 5:20*.

Do not compromise in righteousness—*Psalm 119:3*.

Do not waver back and forth—*1 Kings 18:21; James 1:8*.

No one can serve two masters—*Matthew 6:24*.

CONSULTATION

Do not consult fortunetellers—*2 Kings 17:17*.
Listening makes one wise—*Proverbs 19:20*.
Obtain guidance—*Proverbs 20:18*.
Plans fail for lack of counsel—*Proverbs 15:22*.

CONTENTMENT

Be satisfied with what you have—*Hebrews 13:5*.
Better to be godly and have little—*Psalm 37:16*.
Content with little or a lot—*Philippians 4:11,12*.
Enjoy life—*Ecclesiastes 3:12,13*.
Glad heart makes happy face—*Proverbs 15:13*.
Godliness with contentment—*1 Timothy 6:6,8*.
Just enough to satisfy needs—*Proverbs 30:8*.
Love of money robs contentment—*Ecclesiastes 5:10*.
Those who fear Lord have contentment—*Proverbs 19:23*.

CONTRITE

Broken and repentant heart—*Psalm 34:18; 51:17*.
God heals the brokenhearted—*Psalm 147:3*.
Humble and contrite—*Isaiah 66:2; 1 Peter 5:5*.

CONVERSATION

Do not use foul or abusive language—*Ephesians 4:29*.
Good words come from good heart—*Matthew 12:35*.
Let your conversation be gracious—*Colossians 4:6*.
Let your yes be yes—*Matthew 5:37; James 5:12*.
No dirty language—*Colossians 3:8*.

CONVICTION OF SIN

Awareness of need for salvation—*Acts 16:30*.

Conscience accuses—*Romans 2:15*.
Convicted of sin—*1 Corinthians 14:24*.
Holy Spirit convicts people—*John 16:8-11*.

CORRECTION

Correct in love—*Hebrews 12:6*.
Correct when necessary in the church—*Titus 2:15*.
Do not fail to correct children—*Proverbs 23:13*.
Happy are those God corrects—*Job 5:17; Psalm 94:12*.
Patiently correct—*2 Timothy 4:2*.
Scripture corrects us—*2 Timothy 3:16,17*.

COUNSEL

Heartfelt counsel of a friend—*Proverbs 27:9*.
Many counselors bring success—*Proverbs 15:22*.
The wise listen to others—*Proverbs 12:15*.
Victory depends on many counselors—*Proverbs 24:6*.
With many counselors, there is safety—*Proverbs 11:14*.

COUNTENANCE

Broken heart crushes the spirit—*Proverbs 15:13*.
Glad heart makes happy face—*Proverbs 15:13*.
Gossiping tongue causes anger—*Proverbs 25:23*.
Let the smile of your face shine on us—*Psalm 4:6*.

COURAGE

Be people of courage—*1 Corinthians 16:13*.
Be strong and courageous—*Deuteronomy 31:7,8,23*.
Do not be afraid or discouraged—*1 Chronicles 28:20*.
God did not give us spirit of timidity—*2 Timothy 1:7*.

God gives us boldness—*Psalm 138:3.*
Holy Spirit gives boldness—*Acts 4:29,31.*

COURTESY

Always be kind—*1 Thessalonians 5:15.*
Be considerate—*Romans 15:1-5.*
Be courteous to strangers—*Ruth 2:14-18.*
Do good to enemies—*Luke 6:35.*

COVENANTS

Abrahamic Covenant—*Genesis 12:1-3.*
Davidic Covenant—*2 Samuel 7:5-17.*
Mosaic Covenant—*Exodus 19:3-6; 20–40.*
New Covenant—*Jeremiah 31:31-34.*
Palestinian Covenant—*Deuteronomy 30.*

COVETOUSNESS

Always greedy for more—*Proverbs 21:26.*
Coveting leads to fighting—*James 4:2.*
Coveting violates law of love—*Romans 13:9.*
Do not be lover of money—*1 Timothy 3:3.*
Do not store treasures on earth—*Matthew 6:19.*
Hard for rich person to get into heaven—*Matthew 19:23.*
Lure of wealth—*Matthew 13:22.*
Money lovers never have enough—*Ecclesiastes 5:10.*
No one can serve two masters—*Matthew 6:24.*

COWARDICE

Contagious—*Deuteronomy 20:8.*
Fear of man—*Proverbs 29:25; Galatians 2:12.*

CREATION

All things created by Christ—*John 1:3; Colossians 1:16.*
Creation by God's great power—*Jeremiah 32:17.*
Creation was in six days—*Exodus 20:11.*
Father is source; Son is agent—*1 Corinthians 8:6.*
God alone is Creator—*Isaiah 44:24.*
God spoke and it was done—*Psalm 33:6,9.*
In the beginning God created—*Genesis 1:1.*

CRIME

Crime leads to bloodshed—*Genesis 9:6.*
Crimes emerge in the heart—*Matthew 15:19,20.*
Criminals not inherit kingdom—*1 Corinthians 6:10.*
When crime not punished, people do wrong—
    Ecclesiastes 8:11.

CRITICISM

Do not ignore constructive criticism—*Proverbs 13:18.*
Gentle words bring life and health—*Proverbs 15:4.*
Harsh words stir up anger—*Proverbs 15:1.*
Listen to constructive criticism—*Proverbs 15:31.*
Reckless words pierce soul—*Proverbs 12:18.*
Take log out of own eye first—*Luke 6:41,42.*
Tongue can cut like sharp razor—*Psalm 52:2.*
Tongue can do enormous damage—*James 3:5.*
Valid criticism is treasured—*Proverbs 25:12.*

CROSS

Christ obedient to the cross—*Philippians 2:8.*
Cross was in God's plan—*Acts 2:23.*
Jesus carried cross—*John 19:17.*

CRUCIFIXION

Blindness of crucifiers—*Luke 23:34.*
Crucified with Christ—*Galatians 2:20.*
Crucifixion prophesied—*Zechariah 12:10.*
Darkness fell across land—*Matthew 27:45; Luke 23:44.*
Jesus betrayed and crucified—*Matthew 26:2.*
Prediction, Christ's disciples scatter—*Zechariah 13:7.*

CULTS

Blinded by Satan—*2 Corinthians 4:4.*
Deceived by Satan—*2 Corinthians 11:14.*
Departure from sound doctrine—*2 Timothy 4:3,4.*
Doctrines of demons—*1 Timothy 4:1-3.*
False Christs—*Matthew 24:4,5,11,24.*
False gods—*1 John 5:21.*
False gospel—*Galatians 1:6-8.*
False prophets, false teachers—*2 Peter 2:1-3.*
Scripture twisting—*Jeremiah 7:8.*
Strange teachings—*Hebrews 13:9.*
Wandering away from truth—*2 Timothy 2:17,18.*

DANCING

A time to dance—*Ecclesiastes 3:4.*
Mourning turns into joyful dancing—*Psalm 30:11.*
Praise God with dancing—*Psalm 149:3; 150:4.*

DANGER, PROTECTION FROM

Angel of the Lord encamps around us—*Psalm 34:7.*
Dwell in secret place of Most High—*Psalm 91:1.*
Fear no evil—*Psalm 23:4.*
God is our hiding place—*Psalm 32:7.*
God's angels watch over us—*Psalm 91:11.*
Lord delivers us out of trouble—*Psalm 34:17-19; 121:8.*

DARKNESS

God called darkness "night"—*Genesis 1:5.*
Minds full of darkness—*Ephesians 4:18.*
No harmony between light and darkness—
  2 Corinthians 6:14,15.
Our hearts were once full of darkness—*Ephesians 5:8.*

DAY

God called the light "day"—*Genesis 1:5.*
Like a thousand years to the Lord—*2 Peter 3:8.*
Six days work—*Exodus 20:9.*

DEAD PEOPLE

Believers go to be with Lord—*Philippians 1:23.*
Unbelievers go to a place of suffering—*Luke 16:19-31.*

DEAFNESS

Lord makes one hear or not hear—*Exodus 4:11.*

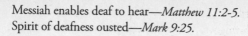

Messiah enables deaf to hear—*Matthew 11:2-5*.
Spirit of deafness ousted—*Mark 9:25*.

DEATH

After death comes judgment—*Hebrews 9:27*.
All people die—*Job 30:23; Ecclesiastes 7:2*.
Breath ceases—*Genesis 49:33*.
Death of saints precious to Lord—*Psalm 116:15*.
Death promised for disobedience—*Genesis 2:16,17*.
Death resulted from sin—*Romans 5:12*.
Fear not walking through valley of death—*Psalm 23:4*.
Foolish people do not plan for death—*Luke 12:20*.
God takes no pleasure in death of wicked—*Ezekiel 18:23; 33:11*.
God will do away with death—*Isaiah 25:8*.
Jesus holds keys of death and Hades—*Revelation 1:18*.
Joining one's ancestors—*Deuteronomy 31:16*.
King of terrors—*Job 18:14*.
Last enemy to be destroyed—*1 Corinthians 15:26*.
No more death—*Revelation 21:3,4*.
No man has power over day of death—*Ecclesiastes 8:8*.
Return to the ground—*Genesis 3:19*.
Sting of death—*1 Corinthians 15:56*.
Time to die—*Ecclesiastes 3:1,2*.
To live is Christ; to die is gain—*Philippians 1:21*.
Wages of sin is death—*Romans 6:23*.

As Judgment

Ananias and Sapphira—*Acts 5:1-10*.
Human race—*Genesis 6:7*.
Saul—*1 Chronicles 10:13*.

Desired

Growing weary in present bodies—*2 Corinthians 5:2*.
Job disgusted with life—*Job 7:15,16; 10:1*.
Jonah yearns for death—*Jonah 4:3,8*.
Paul would rather be with the Lord—*2 Corinthians 5:8*.

Exemption from

Christians will be raptured—*1 Thessalonians 4:17*.
Elijah taken to heaven—*2 Kings 2:1*.
Enoch taken to heaven—*Genesis 5:24; Hebrews 11:5*.

Intermediate State

At home with Lord—*2 Corinthians 5:8*.
Depart and be with Christ—*Philippians 1:21,23,24*.
In paradise—*Luke 23:43*.
Souls under God's altar—*Revelation 6:9,10*.

Of Righteous

Better to be away from body—*2 Corinthians 5:8*.
Blessed are those who die in the Lord—*Revelation 14:13*.
Dying is better—*Philippians 1:21-23*.
Entrusting spirit into God's hand—*Psalm 31:5*.
Falling asleep—*John 11:11*.
God will snatch us from power of death—*Psalm 49:15*.
Godly who die will rest in peace—*Isaiah 57:2*.
Not all of us will die—*1 Corinthians 15:51*.
Our death is precious to God—*Psalm 116:15*.
When we die, we go to be with the Lord— *Romans 14:8*.
Will receive an eternal body—*2 Corinthians 5:1*.

Of Wicked

God cuts off the godless—*Job 27:8.*
Wicked do not anticipate death—*Luke 12:20.*
Wicked will be destroyed—*Proverbs 2:22.*
Years of the wicked are cut short—*Proverbs 10:27.*

Preparation for

Be mindful of how brief time is on earth—*Psalm 39:4.*
In life and death, we belong to Lord—*Romans 14:8.*
Make the most of your time on earth—*Psalm 90:12.*
Set your affairs in order—*2 Kings 20:1.*
We look forward to city in heaven—*Hebrews 13:14.*

DEBT

No excessive interest—*Exodus 22:25.*
Pay debts—*Deuteronomy 24:14,15; Romans 13:8.*
Refusal to go into debt—*Genesis 14:22-24.*

DECEIT/DECEPTION

Do not be deceived—*Colossians 2:4.*
False apostles deceive—*2 Corinthians 11:13.*
False witness tells lies—*Proverbs 12:17.*
Human heart is most deceitful—*Jeremiah 17:9.*
Keep lips from telling lies—*1 Peter 3:10.*
Lord detests deceivers—*Psalm 5:6.*
Many deceivers in the world—*2 John 1:7.*
Satan deceives—*Genesis 3:4.*

DECISIONS, GUIDING PRINCIPLES OF

Ask for God's wisdom—*1 Samuel 14:36-41; James 1:5.*
Many counselors bring success—*Proverbs 15:22.*

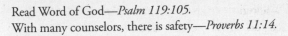

Read Word of God—*Psalm 119:105*.

With many counselors, there is safety—*Proverbs 11:14*.

DEMONS

Can inflict physical pain—*2 Corinthians 12:7*.

Destiny is Lake of Fire—*Matthew 25:41*.

Doctrines of—*1 Timothy 4:1-3*.

Evil spirits—*Luke 10:19,20*.

Fallen angels—*Matthew 12:24-28*.

Lying spirits—*1 Timothy 4:1*.

Many can be present in one person—*Luke 8:30*.

Scream as they leave victims—*Acts 8:7*.

Some are presently confined—*2 Peter 2:4*.

Some committed unnatural sin—*Genesis 6:2-4*.

Some did not keep their first estate—*Jude 6*.

Tormenting spirit—*1 Samuel 16:14; 18:10; 19:9*.

DEPENDABILITY

Faithful in small matters—*Luke 16:10*.

Faithful to the end—*Hebrews 3:14*.

Remain faithful—*2 Timothy 3:14*.

Stand true to what you believe—*1 Corinthians 16:13*.

Stay true to the Lord—*Philippians 1:27*.

DEPRAVITY OF MAN

All have sinned—*Romans 3:23*.

Born a sinner—*Psalm 51:5*.

From human heart comes evil—*Mark 7:21*.

Hearts full of darkness—*Ephesians 5:8*.

Human heart is most deceitful—*Jeremiah 17:9*.

Not a single person who never sins—*Ecclesiastes 7:20*.

Sinful nature loves to do evil—*Galatians 5:17*.

DEPRESSION

Broken heart—*Psalm 34:18; Proverbs 17:22*.
Can result from failure to confess—*Psalm 32:3,4*.
Can result from guilt—*Genesis 4:6,7*.
God is with you through deep waters—*2 Samuel 22:17*.
God of all comfort helps us—*2 Corinthians 1:3,7*.
Trust God in times of trouble—*Psalm 50:15*.
We are pressed, but not crushed—*2 Corinthians 4:8*.

DESIRE

Avoid shameful desires—*Colossians 3:5*.
Captive to desires—*2 Timothy 3:6*.
Desire for God—*Psalm 73:25; Isaiah 26:9*.
Desire for things of world—*1 John 2:15,16*.
Desires are known to God—*Psalm 38:9*.
Do not chase evil desires—*1 Peter 4:2,3*.
God fulfills desires of those who fear Him—*Psalm 145:19*.
Thirst for God—*Psalm 42:1,2; 63:1; 143:6; Amos 8:11*.

DEVOTIONS

All-night prayer—*1 Samuel 15:11; Psalm 55:17; 119:62*.
New strength every morning—*Isaiah 33:2*.
Pray day and night—*Luke 2:37; 1 Thessalonians 3:10*.
Pray privately—*Matthew 6:5,6*.
Prayer in the morning—*Psalm 5:3; 119:147*.

DEVOUT

Do all for glory of God—*1 Corinthians 10:31*.

Do not look back—*Luke 9:62.*

✘ Honor God with body—*1 Corinthians 6:20.*

Live to please God—*1 Thessalonians 4:1.*

Live worthy of God—*1 Thessalonians 2:12.*

Living sacrifice—*Romans 12:1.*

Love Lord with whole heart—*Luke 10:27.*

No halfhearted commitment—*Matthew 6:24.*

Offer yourselves to God—*Romans 6:13.*

✘ Sacrifice everything—*Luke 14:33.*

Serve God in holiness—*Luke 1:74,75.*

DIET

Body is temple of Holy Spirit—*1 Corinthians 6:19.*

Do not make stomach a god—*Philippians 3:19.*

Eat, drink, and be merry—*Ecclesiastes 5:18.*

Restraint in eating—*Proverbs 23:2,20,21; 25:16.*

Subdue the body—*1 Corinthians 9:27.*

Vegetarian and nonvegetarian—*Romans 14:2.*

DILIGENCE

Be strong and steady—*1 Corinthians 15:58.*

Diligently obey commands of Lord—*Deuteronomy 6:17.*

Do not tire of doing good—*Galatians 6:9.*

Guard heart, for it affects everything—*Proverbs 4:23.*

Never forget what Lord has done—*Deuteronomy 4:9.*

Strain to reach end of race—*Philippians 3:14.*

Whatever you do, do well—*Ecclesiastes 9:10.*

DISAGREEMENT

Avoid disputes—*Proverbs 17:14.*

Settle disputes—*1 Corinthians 6:1-7.*

Stay away from arguing—*Philippians 2:14*.

Stop arguing—*1 Corinthians 1:10*.

DISAPPOINTMENT

Cast burdens on Lord—*Psalm 55:22*.

Hope in God—*Psalm 43:5*.

Let not your heart be troubled—*John 14:27*.

We are troubled but not distressed—*2 Corinthians 4:8,9*.

DISCERNMENT

Discerning of spirits—*1 John 4:1-6; Revelation 2:2*.

Importance of discernment—*Job 12:11*.

Lack of discernment—*Psalm 82:5; 92:6; Romans 3:11*.

Prayer for discerning heart—*Psalm 119:125*.

Spiritual man discerns—*1 Corinthians 2:14-16*.

Word of God helps us discern—*Acts 17:11*.

DISCIPLES AND DISCIPLESHIP

Bear fruit—*John 15:8*.

Do not lose race—*Philippians 2:16*.

Influence world as salt—*Matthew 5:13*.

Jesus must be above family—*Luke 14:26*.

Leave all for Jesus—*Luke 14:33*.

Listen to Jesus—*John 10:27*.

Love God with whole heart—*Deuteronomy 6:5*.

Make disciples—*Matthew 28:18-20*.

Run so that you will win—*1 Corinthians 9:24*.

Self-denial—*Matthew 16:24*.

Steadfast in commitment—*John 8:31*.

DISCIPLINE FROM GOD

Blessed are those God corrects—*Job 5:17; Psalm 94:12*.

✝ Do not ignore the Lord's discipline—*Proverbs 3:11,12*.

⚔God disciplines with sickness and pain—*Job 33:19*.
God disciplines those He loves—*Proverbs 3:12*.
Lord can discipline severely—*Psalm 118:18*.
✘ Lord disciplines because we need it—*Psalm 119:75*.

DISCOURAGEMENT, OVERCOMING

Be of good cheer—*John 16:33*.
Be of good courage—*Joshua 1:9*.
Go boldly to throne of grace—*Hebrews 4:16*.
Have confidence in prayer requests—*1 John 5:14*.
Let not your heart be troubled—*John 14:27*.
Wait on the Lord—*Psalm 27:14*.

DISEASE

Caused by evil spirit—*Luke 13:10-16*.
Caused by Satan—*Job 2:6,7*.
Caused by sin—*Leviticus 26:14-16; John 5:14*.
Disobedience brings—*Deuteronomy 28:21,22*.
Divine discipline—*Psalm 51:8*.
Famine and disease—*Jeremiah 29:17; Ezekiel 5:17*.
God can prevent—*Exodus 15:26*.
God heals our diseases—*Psalm 103:3*.
Hope deferred makes heart sick—*Proverbs 13:12*.
Jesus heals—*Matthew 4:23,24; 14:14; Luke 4:40*.
Prayer of faith shall save the sick—*James 5:15,16*.
Suffering illness has some value—*James 1:2-4,12*.

DISHONESTY

Do not cheat anyone—*Leviticus 19:13*.
Do not use dishonest standards—*Leviticus 19:35*.
Lord despises double standards—*Proverbs 20:10*.

Lord hates cheating—*Proverbs 11:1*.
Never cheat Christian brother—*1 Thessalonians 4:6*.

DISOBEDIENCE

Brings punishment—*Isaiah 42:24,25*.
Death promised—*Genesis 2:16,17*.
Disobey, be least in kingdom—*Matthew 5:19*.
Disobey, God withholds blessing—*Deuteronomy 11:17*.
God angry at—*1 Samuel 28:18; Ephesians 5:6*.
Warnings against—*Deuteronomy 28:15-68*.

DIVORCE

Bound together until death separates—*Romans 7:1-3*.
God hates divorce—*Malachi 2:16*.
God permitted because of men's hard hearts—*Matthew 19:7,8*.
Marital unfaithfulness and divorce—*Matthew 5:31,32*.
Paul's instruction on divorce—*1 Corinthians 7:10-13*.
Reconciliation the better way—*Romans 12:18*.

DOCTRINE

Be nourished by—*1 Timothy 4:6*.
Correctly explain the Word—*2 Timothy 2:15*.
Do not be carried away by strange teachings—*Hebrews 13:9*.
Do not distort Word of God—*2 Corinthians 4:2*.
Do not forsake teaching—*Proverbs 4:2*.
Do not tolerate false teachers—*2 John 10*.
Doctrinal disagreement—*1 Corinthians 1:10-17*.
Doctrines of demons—*1 Timothy 4:1-3*.

Encourage by sound doctrine—*Titus 1:9.*
False teachers deceive—*Matthew 24:5.*
Preach the Word—*Mark 16:15,16; 1 Timothy 4:2,13.*
Teach doctrine—*1 Timothy 4:6.*
Teach sound doctrine—*Titus 2:1.*

DOUBT

Doubting Thomas—*John 20:25-29.*
Even small faith brings big miracles—*Matthew 17:20.*
O you of little faith—*Matthew 6:30; 8:25,26; 14:31.*

DRESS

Adam and Eve ashamed at nakedness—*Genesis 3:7.*
Do not be concerned about outward beauty—
    1 Peter 3:3.
Man must not wear women's clothing—*Deuteronomy
    22:5.*
Woman must not wear men's clothing—*Deuteronomy
    22:5.*

DUTIES OF CHRISTIAN SERVANTS

Announce Kingdom of Heaven—*Matthew 10:7.*
Be a servant—*Mark 10:43.*
Be an example to believers—*1 Timothy 4:12.*
Be Christ's ambassadors—*2 Corinthians 5:20.*
Equip God's people—*Ephesians 4:11,12.*
Fan into a flame your spiritual gift—*2 Timothy 1:6.*
Go and make disciples—*Matthew 28:19,20.*
Please God, not people—*1 Thessalonians 2:4.*
Pray, preach, and teach—*Acts 6:4; Ephesians 6:20.*
Take God's message everywhere—*Acts 22:15.*

DUTY OF MAN TO GOD

Fear God, do His will—*Deuteronomy 10:12*.
Love God completely—*Deuteronomy 6:5*.
Obey God's commands—*Joshua 22:5*.
Walk humbly with God—*Micah 6:8*.

EARTH

Earth is the Lord's—*1 Samuel 2:8*.

God created heavens and earth—*Isaiah 45:18*.

God gave earth to man—*Psalm 115:16*.

God placed world on its foundation—*Psalm 104:5*.

Ground of earth cursed—*Genesis 3:17*.

New heavens, new earth—*Isaiah 65:17; Revelation 21:1*.

EARTHQUAKES

Earthquake, prisoners freed—*Acts 16:26*.

Earthquake, Christ's tomb—*Matthew 28:2*.

Earthquakes in many parts of world—*Matthew 24:7*.

Greatest earthquake—*Revelation 16:18*.

Mount of Olives will split apart—*Zechariah 14:4*.

Sixth seal judgment—*Revelation 6:12*.

EASTER

Christ's resurrection, gospel—*1 Corinthians 15:1-3*.

First to rise from the dead—*Colossians 1:18*.

He is risen—*Matthew 28:6,7; Mark 16:6*.

If Christ not raised, our faith is in vain—*1 Corinthians 15:17,20*.

ECOLOGICAL CONCERNS

Adam and Eve cultivated Garden—*Genesis 2:8,15*.

Barren land—*Deuteronomy 29:23*.

Bitter water—*Exodus 15:23-25*.

Do not destroy trees—*Deuteronomy 20:19,20*.

Earth defiled—*Isaiah 24:5*.

Earth will wear out—*Isaiah 51:6.*

Fields ruined—*2 Kings 3:19.*

Forest destroyed—*Isaiah 10:18; James 3:5.*

Land cries out—*Job 31:38.*

EDEN

Cherubim guards—*Genesis 3:24.*

Garden in Eden—*Genesis 2:8.*

God banished Adam and Eve from—*Genesis 3:23.*

EDUCATION

Holy Spirit is our teacher—*John 14:26.*

Knowledge can make one prideful—*1 Corinthians 8:1.*

✗ Knowledge is better than wealth—*Ecclesiastes 7:12.*

Learn from personal experience—*Psalm 78:1-8.*

✗ Learn from the ants—*Proverbs 6:6.*

Listen to what parents teach—*Proverbs 1:8; 6:20.*

✗ Pray for God to give wisdom—*James 1:5.*

Teach children about God—*Deuteronomy 4:10; 11:19.*

ELECTION

Chosen in Christ—*Ephesians 1:4.*

Elect are still responsible to believe—*Acts 13:48.*

Encompasses past through future—*Romans 8:29,30.*

Father draws people to Christ—*John 6:44.*

Father gave believers to Christ—*John 6:37; 17:2,6.*

God chose you—*Deuteronomy 7:6; 2 Thessalonians 2:13.*

God's plan stands firm—*Isaiah 14:26,27.*

Is from all eternity—*Ephesians 1:4; 2 Timothy 1:9.*

Originates in free choice of God—*Ephesians 1:5,6.*

EMOTION

Anger causes quarrels—*Proverbs 30:33.*
Avoid angry people—*Proverbs 22:24,25.*
Be content in any circumstance—*Philippians 4:11,12.*
Cheerful look brings joy—*Proverbs 15:30.*
Devil instigates jealousy—*James 3:14-16.*
Do not bear grudge—*Leviticus 19:18.*
Do not hate for no reason—*Psalm 38:19; 69:4.*
Happy are those who fear the Lord—*Psalm 112:1.*
Happy heart makes face cheerful—*Proverbs 15:13.*
Jealousy is destructive—*Proverbs 27:4.*
Jealousy kills—*Job 5:2.*
Love is not easily angered—*1 Corinthians 13:5.*
Quarreling, jealousy—*2 Corinthians 12:20.*
Restrain anger—*Proverbs 19:11.*
Turn from rage and envy—*Psalm 37:8.*
Watch out for jealousy—*James 4:2.*

EMPLOYEE

Hard workers get rich—*Proverbs 10:4.*
Parable of workers in vineyard—*Matthew 20:1-16.*
Those who work deserve their pay—*Luke 10:7.*
Those who work deserve to be fed—*Matthew 10:10.*
Trustworthy employees—*Titus 2:9,10.*
Work hard and become a leader—*Proverbs 12:24.*
Work six days—*Exodus 23:12; Deuteronomy 5:13.*

EMPLOYER

Be fair—*Job 31:13,14.*
Do not cheat employees of wages—*James 5:4.*
Never take advantage—*Deuteronomy 24:14,15.*

Pay workers promptly—*Leviticus 19:13*.

Treat employees well—*Leviticus 25:43*.

ENCOURAGEMENT

Christians encourage each other—*1 Thessalonians 4:18*.

Comfort from Jesus—*Matthew 14:27*.

Exhortation to encourage each other—*Philippians 2:1,2*.

God encourages us—*2 Corinthians 7:6*.

God's Word encourages us—*Psalm 119:28*.

Kind words cheer people up—*Proverbs 12:25*.

Patiently correct, rebuke—*2 Timothy 4:2*.

Speak encouraging words—*Ephesians 4:29*.

ENDURANCE

Adversity builds endurance—*Romans 5:3,4; James 1:3*.

Endurance is rewarded—*2 Timothy 3:11; James 1:12*.

Endure God's chastening—*Hebrews 12:7*.

Endure suffering—*2 Timothy 2:3*.

Endure to the end—*Matthew 10:22*.

God gives rest to the weary—*Jeremiah 31:25*.

Hope gives endurance—*1 Thessalonians 1:3*.

Patient endurance—*2 Corinthians 1:6; 2 Peter 1:6*.

Patiently endure testing—*James 1:12*.

Patiently endure unfair treatment—*1 Peter 2:19*.

Run with endurance—*Hebrews 12:1*.

ENEMIES

✗ Do not rejoice when enemy falls—*Proverbs 24:17,18*.

Fall into their own traps—*Psalm 57:6*.

Feed hungry enemies—*Proverbs 25:21,22*.

Love your enemies—*Luke 6:27*.

Pray for those who persecute you—*Romans 12:14*.

ENVY

Do not envy evil people—*Psalm 37:1; Proverbs 23:17*.

Do not envy violent people—*Proverbs 3:31*.

Envy emerges in heart—*Mark 7:20-22*.

Envy leads to evil—*James 3:14-16*.

Envy of neighbors harmful—*Ecclesiastes 4:4*.

Envy rooted in sinful nature—*Galatians 5:19-21*.

Envy rots bones—*Proverbs 14:30*.

Love does not envy—*1 Corinthians 13:4*.

Rid yourself of envy—*1 Peter 2:1*.

ETERNAL LIFE

Believers will never perish—*John 10:28*.

Comes through faith in Christ—*John 3:14-16,36; 5:24*.

Eternal life and knowing God—*John 17:3*.

Eternal life in the Son—*1 John 5:11-13,20*.

Gift of God—*Romans 6:23*.

Living water wells up to eternal life—*John 4:14*.

ETERNAL STATE

Better things await us in eternity—*Hebrews 10:34*.

Creation eagerly awaits redemption—*Romans 8:19-21*.

In my Father's house are many rooms—*John 14:2,3*.

Inheritance awaits us—*1 Peter 1:3,4*.

New heaven and new earth—*Revelation 21:1,4*.

No more curse, no more night—*Revelation 22:3-5*.

Our resurrection body lives forever—*2 Corinthians 5:1*.

We will shine—*Daniel 12:3*.

ETERNITY

God inhabits eternity—*Isaiah 57:15*.

God is from eternity to eternity—*Isaiah 43:13*.

God put eternity in human heart—*Ecclesiastes 3:11*.

God's plan is from all eternity—*Ephesians 3:11*.

Jesus is from eternity past—*Micah 5:2*.

EVANGELISM

Commanded of Christ's followers—*Matthew 28:19,20*.

Fishers of men—*Luke 5:10*.

God gives evangelists to church—*Ephesians 4:11*.

Lord does not want anyone to perish—*2 Peter 3:9*.

One lost sheep worthy of finding—*Matthew 18:12-14*.

One plants, another waters—*1 Corinthians 3:6-9*.

Pray for harvesters—*Luke 10:2*.

We are Christ's witnesses—*Luke 24:45-49; Acts 1:8*.

EVIL

Avoid Appearance of

Avoid every kind of evil—*1 Thessalonians 5:22*.

Do not violate another's conscience—*Romans 14:1*.

For Good

Betraying a friend—*Psalm 7:4*.

Repay evil for good—*Psalm 35:12; 109:5*.

Seeking to stone Jesus for His miracles—*John 10:32*.

EVOLUTION

Contradicts creation account—*Genesis 1–2*.

Creation proves a Creator—*Psalm 19:1-4; Hebrews 3:4*.

Design of universe proves Designer—*Romans 1:18-20*.

Human morality proves Moral Source—*Romans 2:14-16*.

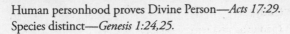

Human personhood proves Divine Person—*Acts 17:29*.
Species distinct—*Genesis 1:24,25*.

EXAMPLE

Christ Is Our

Forgiving—*Colossians 3:13*.
Humility—*Philippians 2:5-11*.
Loving—*John 13:34; Ephesians 5:2*.
Sacrifice for others—*1 John 3:16*.
Self-giving—*2 Corinthians 8:9*.
Servanthood—*Matthew 20:28; Mark 10:43-45*.
Suffering—*1 Peter 2:21*.

Good

Be example by doing good deeds—*Titus 2:7*.
Be example to all believers—*1 Timothy 4:12*.
Leaders lead by good example—*1 Peter 5:3*.

Heavenly Father Is Our

Compassion—*Luke 6:36*.
Holy—*Leviticus 11:44; 19:2*.
Perfect—*Matthew 5:48*.

EXORCISM

Apostles have authority—*Mark 3:14,15*.
Believers cast out demons—*Mark 16:17*.
Jesus cast out demons—*Matthew 4:24; Mark 1:34*.

FAILURE

Christ's strength made perfect in weakness—
2 Corinthians 12:9.

God helps us through failures—*Psalm 34:19,20.*

New mercies every morning—*Lamentations 3:22,23.*

Total life failure—*1 Corinthians 3:15.*

FAITH

Blessed are those who trust—*Jeremiah 17:7.*

Cling tightly to your faith—*1 Timothy 1:19.*

Do not throw away trust—*Hebrews 10:35.*

Faith brings answered prayer—*Matthew 15:28; 21:22.*

Faith grows from hearing God's Word—*Romans 10:17.*

Faith is certainty of what we do not see—*Hebrews 11:1.*

Joy in trusting God—*Psalm 40:4.*

Live by faith, not sight—*2 Corinthians 5:7.*

Miracles through faith—*Matthew 21:21.*

Small faith yields big results—*Luke 17:5,6.*

Tests of faith—*1 Peter 1:7.*

Trust in Lord with whole heart—*Proverbs 3:5.*

Trust in Lord, not man—*Psalm 118:8.*

Without faith, impossible to please God—*Hebrews
11:6.*

FAITHFUL, CHOOSE TO REMAIN

Always be faithful—*Proverbs 3:3.*

Be a faithful servant—*Matthew 25:23.*

Be faithful in prayer—*Romans 12:12.*

Choose today whom you will serve—*Joshua 24:15.*

Faithful in small matters—*Luke 16:10.*
Fruit of the spirit and faithfulness—*Galatians 5:22.*
God preserves the faithful—*Psalm 31:23.*
Hold tightly to hope—*Hebrews 10:23.*
Let us cling to Him—*Hebrews 4:14.*
Lord does not forsake the faithful—*Psalm 37:28.*
Lord guards the faithful—*Psalm 97:10.*
Remain faithful even in face of death—*Revelation 2:10.*

FALL OF MAN

Adam and Eve warned not to disobey—*Genesis 2:17.*
Adam's sin brought condemnation—*Romans 5:18-21.*
Each of us has gone astray—*Isaiah 53:6.*
Each turned to follow downward path—*Ecclesiastes 7:29.*
Eve deceived—*2 Corinthians 11:3.*
In Adam all die—*1 Corinthians 15:22.*
Sin entered entire human race—*Romans 5:12.*

FALSE CHRISTS

Many will arise—*Matthew 24:5-26; Mark 13:6-22.*

FALSE CONFIDENCE

Confidence in powerful people—*Psalm 146:3.*
Do not trust in bow—*Psalm 44:6.*
Do not trust own understanding—*Proverbs 3:5.*
Trust in mere humans—*Isaiah 2:22; Jeremiah 17:5.*
Trust in oneself—*Proverbs 28:26.*
Trust in wealth—*Psalm 49:5,6; Proverbs 11:28.*

FALSE WITNESS

Corrupt witness—*Proverbs 19:28.*

Do not lie—*Leviticus 19:11.*
Do not pass along false reports—*Exodus 23:1.*
Do not testify falsely—*Exodus 20:16; Deuteronomy 5:20.*
From the heart comes lying—*Matthew 15:19.*
Speaks lies—*Proverbs 14:5.*
Will not go unpunished—*Proverbs 19:9; 21:28.*

FALSEHOOD

Abhor falsehood—*Psalm 119:163.*
Constant liars—*Proverbs 6:12-14.*
Corrupt speech—*Proverbs 2:12.*
Evil words—*Proverbs 11:9.*
Expert at telling lies—*Psalm 52:2; Proverbs 12:17.*
Father of lies is devil—*John 8:44.*
Keep lips from telling lies—*Psalm 34:13; Colossians 3:9.*
Lord hates liars—*Proverbs 12:22.*
Lying tongue hates its victims—*Proverbs 26:28.*
Mouths full of lies—*Psalm 50:19; 144:8,11.*
Put away all falsehood—*Ephesians 4:25.*

FAMILY

Family instituted—*Genesis 2:23,24.*
Family may betray you—*Matthew 10:21; Mark 13:12.*
Family quarrels—*Genesis 21:10; Proverbs 18:19; 19:13.*
Jesus must be above family—*Luke 14:26.*
Jesus' true family—*Matthew 12:48,49; Luke 8:21.*
Provide for family—*1 Timothy 5:8.*

FAMINE

Barns and granaries empty—*Joel 1:16,17.*
Death by famine—*Jeremiah 14:15.*

Famine and disease—*Ezekiel 5:17; Luke 21:11.*
Famines and earthquakes—*Matthew 24:7.*
God rescues in times of famine—*Psalm 33:18,19.*
War, famine, and disease—*Jeremiah 29:17.*

FASTING

Do not make a show of it—*Matthew 6:16.*
Fasting and confession of sin—*1 Samuel 7:6.*

FAT (OVERWEIGHT)

Gluttony—*Proverbs 23:2.*
Gorging—*Proverbs 23:20,21.*
Overeating—*Proverbs 25:16.*
Stomach is a god—*Philippians 3:19.*
Take care of body—*1 Corinthians 6:19,20.* ✓

FATHER

Authority of father—*Numbers 30:3-5.*
Even if father forsakes you, God will not—*Psalm 27:10.*
Exemplary fathers—*Genesis 17:18,20; 35:1-5.*
Fatherly discipline—*Proverbs 3:11,12.*
Good children bring joy to father—*Proverbs 23:24.*
Honor father, live long—*Exodus 20:12.*
Influence of good father—*Proverbs 20:7.*
Son listen to father—*Proverbs 1:8; 13:1.*
Striking father—*Exodus 21:15.*

Heavenly

Author of divine plan (decree)—*Psalm 2:7-9.*
Author of election—*Ephesians 1:5,6.*
Cares for the redeemed—*Matthew 7:11.*
Disciplines Christians—*Hebrews 12:9,10.*

Has a set purpose—*Acts 2:23*.

Is the Father of all people—*Acts 17:29*.

Is the Father of believers—*Galatians 4:6*.

Is the Father of Jesus—*Matthew 3:17*.

Keeps us secure in salvation—*John 10:29*.

FEAR

Do not be afraid of sudden fear—*Proverbs 3:25*.

God has not given us spirit of fear—*2 Timothy 1:7*.

If God is for us, who can be against us?—*Romans 8:31*.

Let not your heart be troubled—*John 14:27*.

Whom shall I fear?—*Psalm 27:1*.

Of the Lord

Always act in the fear of the Lord—*2 Chronicles 19:9*.

Angel of the Lord guards all who fear him—*Psalm 34:7*.

Be sure to fear the Lord—*1 Samuel 12:24*.

Beginning of knowledge—*Psalm 111:10; Proverbs 1:7*.

Fear Lord alone—*Deuteronomy 13:4*.

Fear Lord and obey commands—*Deuteronomy 5:29*.

Fear Lord and serve Him—*Deuteronomy 6:13*.

Fear Lord as long as you live—*Deuteronomy 6:2*.

Fear the Lord and turn back on evil—*Proverbs 3:7; 16:6*.

God accepts those who fear Him—*Acts 10:34,35*.

God blesses those who fear Him—*Psalm 115:13*.

God fulfills desires of those who fear Him—*Psalm 145:19*.

God's mercy goes out to those who fear Him—*Luke 1:50*.

FELLOWSHIP

Holy Spirit

Fellowship with Holy Spirit—*2 Corinthians 13:14*.

Holy Spirit our advocate—*John 14:16.*
Spirit of God lives in you—*Romans 8:9*

Of Righteous

Agree wholeheartedly—*Philippians 2:2.*
Be knit together by ties of love—*Colossians 2:2.*
Be of one mind—*1 Corinthians 1:10; 1 Peter 3:8.*
Build up brothers—*Luke 22:32.*
Can two walk together without agreeing?—*Amos 3:3.*
Confess sins to each other—*James 5:16.*
Encourage each other—*1 Thessalonians 4:18; 5:11.*
Love each other—*John 13:34; Hebrews 13:1; 1 John 4:7.*

With Christ

Christ is among you—*2 Corinthians 13:5.*
Christ is the true vine—*John 15:1.*
Christ lives in you—*Romans 8:10; Colossians 1:27.*
Fellowship with Son—*1 Corinthians 1:9; 1 John 2:24,28.*
Joined to the Lord—*1 Corinthians 6:17.*
We are Christ's body—*Romans 12:5.*
Where two or three gather together—*Matthew 18:20.*

With God

God's home will be among His people—*Revelation 21:3.*
Requires obedience to God's commands—*1 John 3:24.*
Those who love Jesus are loved by Father—*John 14:23.*

With Wicked

Avoid divisive people—*Romans 16:17.*
Do not fellowship with sinners—*1 Corinthians 5:11.*
Do not spend time with liars—*Psalm 26:4.*
Do not team up with unbelievers—*2 Corinthians 6:14.*

Make no treaties with evil people—*Deuteronomy 7:2*.

Separate from pagans—*Ezra 10:11*.

Stay away from evil people—*Numbers 16:26; Proverbs 1:10*.

Stay away from fools—*Proverbs 14:7*.

Stay away from idle—*2 Thessalonians 3:6*.

FIGHT OF FAITH

Fight the good fight—*1 Timothy 6:12*.

Paul fought good fight—*2 Timothy 4:7*.

FINANCE

Bad financial planning—*Luke 12:16-21; 14:28-30*.

Be honest in financial dealings—*Proverbs 11:1*.

Do not build up treasure on earth—*Matthew 6:19-21*.

Do not owe anyone anything—*Romans 13:8*.

Generosity brings blessing—*Proverbs 22:9*.

Give money to the poor—*Matthew 19:21; 1 John 3:17*.

Good financial planning—*Genesis 41:34-36*.

Provide for family—*1 Timothy 5:8*.

Share money generously—*Romans 12:8*.

Trust God, not money—*1 Timothy 6:17*.

Trust in money and down you go—*Proverbs 11:28*.

Use money for good—*1 Timothy 6:18*.

Watch out for love of money—*1 Timothy 6:10*.

We are stewards of what God gives us—*Luke 16:1-13*.

FIRE

Burning bush—*Exodus 3:2*.

Eternal fire prepared for devil—*Matthew 25:41*.

Lake of fire—*Revelation 21:8*.

Lord descended on Mount Sinai in fire—*Exodus 19:18*.

Pillar of fire—*Exodus 13:21,22*.
Tongues of fire—*Acts 2:3*.

FIRSTBORN

Christ as firstborn—*Colossians 1:15*.
Dedicate firstborn to God—*Exodus 13:2,12,13,15*.
Firstborn from the dead—*Revelation 1:5*.
Firstborn sons in Egypt will die—*Exodus 11:5*.
Redemption of firstborn—*Exodus 22:29,30*.

FLATTERY

Enticed by flattery—*Proverbs 7:21*.
Flattering lips—*Psalm 12:2*.
Flattery causes ruin—*Proverbs 26:28*.
Flattery lays a trap—*Proverbs 29:5*.
Flattery of an adulterous woman—*Proverbs 7:5*.

FLOOD

Destroyed all living creatures—*Genesis 6:13,17*.
God said no more floods—*Isaiah 54:9*.

FOOD

Breakfast—*Judges 19:5*.
Do not let stomach become a god—*Philippians 3:19*.
Do not overeat—*Proverbs 23:1-3*.
Evening meal—*Genesis 24:25,33*.
Feeding 5,000—*Matthew 14:15-21*.
Food eaten by angels—*Genesis 19:1-3*.
Fruit—*Amos 8:2*.
Locusts—*Matthew 3:4*.
Manna—*Psalm 78:25*.

- Meat—*Genesis 9:3; 1 Kings 4:22,23.*
- Vegetables—*Numbers 11:5.*

From God

For every living thing—*Psalm 136:25.*
From the earth—*Psalm 104:14.*
Grasses and other green plants—*Genesis 1:30.*
Seed-bearing plants—*Genesis 1:29.*

FOOL

Constant quarrels—*Proverbs 18:6.*
Does not save money—*Proverbs 21:20.*
Enjoys doing wrong—*Proverbs 10:23.*
Gives full vent to anger—*Proverbs 29:11.*
Invites trouble—*Proverbs 10:14.*
Misuses mouth—*Proverbs 18:7.*
Refuses to work—*Ecclesiastes 4:5.*
Says there is no God—*Psalm 14:1; 53:1.*

FORGIVE OTHERS

Forgive and be forgiven—*Luke 6:37.*
Forgive as you have been forgiven—*Ephesians 4:32.*
Forgive one another—*Matthew 6:12,14; Ephesians 4:32.*
Forgive without measure—*Matthew 18:21,22.*

FORGIVENESS

Of Enemies

Do not repay evil for evil—*Romans 12:17,19.*
Love your enemy—*Matthew 5:43,44; Luke 6:27.*
Turn the other cheek—*Matthew 5:39.*

Of Sins

Blessedness of forgiveness—*Psalm 32:1.*

Confess your sins, God forgives—*1 John 1:9*.
God forgives our iniquities—*Psalm 103:3*.
Jesus forgives—*Matthew 9:2-6*.
Those who confess sins find mercy—*Proverbs 28:13*.

FORTUNETELLING

Do not listen to fortunetellers—*Jeremiah 27:9*.
Do not practice fortunetelling—*Leviticus 19:26*.
No more fortunetellers—*Micah 5:12*.

FRIENDSHIP

Avoid friendship with world—*James 4:4*.
Can two walk together if not agreed?—*Amos 3:3*.
Do not forsake friend—*Proverbs 27:10*.
Earnest counsel from friend—*Proverbs 27:9*.
Friend closer than brother—*Proverbs 18:24*.
Friend loves at all times—*Proverbs 17:17*.
Gossip separates friends—*Proverbs 16:28*.
Lay down life for friends—*John 15:13*.
Wounds from a friend—*Proverbs 27:6*.
You are Christ's friend if you obey—*John 15:14*.

FUNERAL

Embalming—*Genesis 50:2,3*.
Funeral procession—*Genesis 50:7-9; Luke 7:12*.
Mourning—*1 Samuel 25:1*.

GAMBLING

Destructive lifestyle—*1 Timothy 6:9*.
Rooted in covetousness—*Luke 12:15; Philippians 2:3,4*.

GAMES, SPIRITUAL

Boxer—*1 Corinthians 9:26*.
Do not lose race—*Philippians 2:16*.
Fight a good fight—*2 Timothy 4:7*.
In race, one gets prize—*1 Corinthians 9:24*.
Run with endurance—*Hebrews 12:1*.

GENEROSITY

All goes well for the generous—*Psalm 112:5*.
Christ sets example—*2 Corinthians 8:9*.
Exhortations to—*1 Corinthians 16:1; 1 Timothy 6:17,18*.
Generous man is happy—*Proverbs 22:9*.
Give generously to others in need—*Ephesians 4:28*.

GIFTS FROM GOD

Spiritual

Bread from heaven—*John 6:32*.
Eternal life—*Acts 11:18*.
Gift of God's Son—*John 3:16*.
Living water—*John 4:10*.

Temporal

Food, drink, and clothes—*Psalm 136:25; 145:15*.
Rain—*Leviticus 26:4; Isaiah 30:23; Zechariah 10:1*.
Riches, wealth, and honor—*2 Chronicles 1:12*.

Giving, Advice on

Do not do publicly—*Matthew 6:1.*
Give money to the poor—*Deuteronomy 15:7,8.*
Give to those in need—*Luke 11:41; 12:33.*
Give to those who ask—*Matthew 5:42.*
Give what you are able—*2 Corinthians 8:12.*
Share food with the hungry—*Isaiah 58:7.*

Glorifying God

Glorify God in death—*John 21:19.*
Glorify God through gifts—*2 Corinthians 9:13.*
Glorify God's name forever—*Psalm 86:12.*

Gluttony

Command against—*Romans 13:13,14.*
Consequence of—*Proverbs 23:21.*
Danger of—*Luke 12:45,46.*
Do not let stomach be a god—*Philippians 3:19.*
Warning against—*Proverbs 23:2,3.*

God

Access to

Approach with confidence—*Hebrews 4:16.*
Close to all who call on Him—*Psalm 145:18.*
Come boldly—*Hebrews 4:16; 10:19.*
Draw near—*James 4:8.*
Through Jesus—*John 14:6; Romans 5:2; Ephesians 2:13.*

Creator

Created all things—*Psalm 89:11; Isaiah 44:24.*
Created heaven and earth—*Genesis 1:1,21.*
Created male and female—*Genesis 5:1,2.*

Father created all through Son—*1 Corinthians 8:6.*
God spoke world into existence—*Psalm 33:9; 148:5.*

Eternality of

Alpha and Omega—*Revelation 1:8.*
Everlasting—*Deuteronomy 33:27.*
First and the Last—*Isaiah 44:6; 48:12.*
From eternity to eternity—*Isaiah 43:13.*
From everlasting to everlasting—*Psalm 90:2.*

Existence of

Existence of world proves God's—*Romans 1:18-20.*
God's law in human heart proves—*Romans 1:19.*
God's provisions testify to His existence—*Acts 14:17.*
Heavens declare glory of God—*Psalm 19:1.*

Faithfulness of

Even when we are not faithful—*2 Timothy 2:13.*
Every promise fulfilled—*Joshua 23:14.*
Faithful in every way—*Psalm 89:1,2,8.*
Faithfulness to each generation—*Psalm 100:5.*
Unfailing faithfulness—*Psalm 25:10.*

Fatherhood of

Father created—*1 Corinthians 8:6.*
Father disciplines us as children—*Hebrews 12:9,10.*
Father to the fatherless—*Psalm 68:5.*
Pray to the Father—*Matthew 6:9.*

Foreknowledge of

Foreknew His people—*Romans 8:29.*
Foretells future, unlike false gods—*Isaiah 42:9; 44:7.*
Only God knows future—*Isaiah 46:9,10.*

Glory of

Dwells in unapproachable light—*1 Timothy 6:16*.
Glory filled tabernacle—*Exodus 40:34*.
Glory on mountaintop—*Exodus 24:17*.
God will not give glory to another—*Isaiah 42:8*.
Illuminates eternal city—*Revelation 21:23*.
Moses' face glowed from God's glory—*Exodus 34:29*.
Son reflects God's own glory—*Hebrews 1:3*.

Goodness of

Give thanks, for God is good—*1 Chronicles 16:34*.
God is good—*Psalm 25:8; 86:5; 100:5; 106:1; 119:68*.
Good to all people—*Psalm 145:8,9*.
Good to those who hope in Him—*Lamentations 3:25*.
Taste and see—*Psalm 34:8*.

Grace of

Abounds for every need—*2 Corinthians 9:8*.
By grace we are saved—*Ephesians 2:8,9; Titus 2:11*.
Empowers us for service—*1 Corinthians 3:10*.
Finding grace at God's throne—*Hebrews 4:16*.
Gives grace to humble—*Proverbs 3:34; 1 Peter 5:5*.
Justification by grace—*Romans 3:24*.
Sufficiency of God's grace—*1 Corinthians 15:10*.
Unmerited favor—*Romans 4:16; Romans 9:16; Titus 3:5*.

Holiness of

Be holy because God is holy—*Leviticus 11:44; 19:2*.
Cannot be tempted by evil—*James 1:13*.
God alone is holy—*1 Samuel 6:20; Psalm 99:9*.
God is light, no darkness—*1 John 1:5*.

God's name is holy—*Psalm 99:3; Isaiah 57:15.*
Holy, holy, holy—*Isaiah 6:3; Revelation 4:8.*

Immutability of
God does not change—*Malachi 3:6.*
God does not change mind—*Numbers 23:19.*
God endures—*Psalm 102:25-27.*
God's purpose will stand—*Psalm 33:11; Isaiah 46:10.*

Impartiality of
Has no favorites—*Romans 2:11; Colossians 3:25.*
Shows no partiality—*Deuteronomy 10:17; Acts 10:34.*

Incomprehensible
God's thoughts higher than ours—*Isaiah 55:8,9.*
Who can know?—*1 Corinthians 2:16.*

Independent
Needs no counsel—*Romans 11:34,35.*
Needs no help—*Isaiah 44:24; Acts 17:25.*

Infinite
High above all nations—*Psalm 113:4-6.*
Highest heavens cannot contain Him—*1 Kings 8:27.*
His greatness is unsearchable—*Psalm 145:3.*

Invisible
Invisible—*Colossians 1:15; Hebrews 11:27.*
No one has seen Him—*John 1:18; 1 Timothy 6:16.*

Jealous
Do not worship other gods—*Exodus 20:5; 34:14.*
God is a jealous God—*Deuteronomy 4:24.*

Judge

Almighty Judge—*Job 34:17.*
Judge in righteousness—*Psalm 7:11.*
Judge of all the earth—*Genesis 18:25.*
Judges with equity—*Psalm 96:10.*
Will judge men's secrets—*Romans 2:16.*

Just

Deals with earth justly—*Genesis 18:25.*
Justice is foundation of His throne—*Psalm 89:14.*

Kindness of

Everlasting kindness—*Isaiah 54:8.*
Full of lovingkindness—*Jeremiah 31:3.*
Kindness in Jesus Christ—*Ephesians 2:6,7.*

Knowledge of

Carefully watches—*Job 34:21; Proverbs 15:3; Psalm 11:4.*
Examines deepest thoughts—*Jeremiah 11:20; 20:12.*
Examines secret motives—*Proverbs 16:2; Jeremiah 17:10.*
Knows all hearts—*Proverbs 21:2; 24:12; Romans 8:27.*
Knows all secrets—*Matthew 6:4,18.*

Love of

Abounds in love—*Psalm 86:5.*
Demonstrated love in sending Jesus—*John 3:16.*
Everlasting love—*Jeremiah 31:3.*
God is love—*1 John 4:8,16.*
God's love endures forever—*1 Chronicles 16:34.*
Nothing can separate us—*Romans 8:38,39.*
Unfailing love—*Psalm 130:7; Isaiah 54:10.*

Mercy of

Father of mercies—*2 Corinthians 1:3*.

Merciful and compassionate—*Deuteronomy 4:31*.

New mercies every morning—*Lamentations 3:22-24*.

Omnipotence of

Incomparably great power—*Ephesians 1:19,20*.

No one can hold back God's hand—*Daniel 4:35*.

No one can reverse God—*Isaiah 43:13*.

No one can thwart God—*Isaiah 14:27*.

Nothing is impossible with God—*Matthew 19:26*.

Nothing too difficult for God—*Genesis 18:14*.

Omnipresence of

God is everywhere—*Psalm 139:2-12*.

Highest heaven cannot contain Him—*1 Kings 8:27*.

In heaven and earth—*Psalm 113:4-6; Isaiah 66:1*.

In Him we live and move and exist—*Acts 17:27,28*.

Omniscience of

Counts and names all stars—*Psalm 147:4,5*.

Declares end from beginning—*Isaiah 46:9,10*.

Eyes penetrate all things—*Hebrews 4:13*.

Knows all about us—*Psalm 139:1-4*.

Knows all outcomes—*Matthew 11:21*.

Knows all things—*1 John 3:20*.

Knows secrets of the heart—*Psalm 44:21*.

Understands every intent—*1 Chronicles 28:9*.

Patience of

Forbearance—*Romans 2:4*.

Slow to anger—*Exodus 34:6; Numbers 14:18*.

Waits patiently for people to be saved—*2 Peter 3:15*.

Perfection of

Father is perfect—*Matthew 5:48*.

His way is perfect—*2 Samuel 22:31*.

His work is perfect—*Deuteronomy 32:4*.

Power of

Everything is possible with God—*Mark 10:27*.

God of miracles—*Job 9:10; Psalm 77:14*.

Has power to do as He pleases—*Psalm 135:6*.

His power is absolute—*Psalm 147:5*.

Nothing is too hard for God—*Jeremiah 32:17,27*.

Presence of

God lives with the humble—*Isaiah 57:15*.

In God we live and move and exist—*Acts 17:28*.

No one can escape from God's spirit—*Psalm 139:7*.

Righteousness of

Commands are righteous—*Psalm 119:172*.

Does no wrong—*Deuteronomy 32:4*.

Judges world in righteousness—*Acts 17:31*.

Savior

God is a God who saves—*Psalm 68:20*.

Lord alone is Savior—*Isaiah 43:11*.

Our God and Savior—*Psalm 27:9; 38:22; 42:11*.

Self-Existent

Has life within Himself—*John 5:26*.

"I Am"—God's name—*Exodus 3:14*.

Sovereign

Above all rule and authority—*Ephesians 1:20-22*.

Enthroned over all—*Isaiah 40:21-26*.

Eternal dominion—*Daniel 4:34,35.*

Every knee will bow before God—*Romans 14:11.*

His plans alone stand—*Psalm 33:8-11; Isaiah 46:10.*

His sovereignty rules over all—*Psalm 103:19.*

King over the earth—*Psalm 47:2.*

Lord does whatever pleases Him—*Psalm 135:6.*

Lord is enthroned as King forever—*Psalm 29:10.*

Lord is God in heaven and earth—*Deuteronomy 4:39.*

Most High over all the earth—*Psalm 83:18.*

Rules all nations—*2 Chronicles 20:6.*

Rules forever—*Exodus 15:18; Psalm 9:7; Revelation 1:6.*

Rules over all things—*Deuteronomy 10:14.*

Spirit

God is invisible—*1 Timothy 1:17.*

God is Spirit—*John 4:24.*

No one has seen or can see God—*1 Timothy 6:15,16.*

Trinity

Baptism in name of Father, Son, Spirit—*Matthew 28:19.*

Benediction mentions—*2 Corinthians 13:14.*

Father, Messiah, and Spirit mentioned—*Isaiah 48:16.*

God is one—*James 2:19.*

God said, "Let *us* go down and confuse their language"—*Genesis 11:7.*

God said, "Man has now become like one of *us*"—*Genesis 3:22.*

God said, "Who will go for *us?*"—*Isaiah 6:8.*

Holy, holy, holy is the Lord—*Isaiah 6:3; Revelation 4:8.*

Jesus baptized, Father speaks, Spirit descends—*Matthew 3:16,17.*

Lord is one—*Deuteronomy 6:4.*
One Spirit, one Lord, one Father—*Ephesians 4:4-6.*

True

All God's words are true—*Psalm 33:4; 119:160.*
Cannot lie—*Numbers 23:19; Titus 1:2.*
Commands are true—*Psalm 119:151.*
God is true—*1 John 5:20.*
True God—*Jeremiah 10:10; John 17:3.*

Unity

God is one—*James 2:19.*
Lord is one—*Deuteronomy 6:4.*
Lord our God is one Lord—*Mark 12:29.*

Wise

Full of wisdom and understanding—*Proverbs 3:19.*
Possesses full understanding—*Job 12:13.*
The only wise God—*Romans 16:27.*

Works of

His work is perfect—*Deuteronomy 32:4.*
How amazing are deeds of Lord—*Psalm 111:2,4.*
How awesome are God's deeds—*Psalm 66:3.*
Many miracles—*Psalm 40:5.*

GODLESSNESS

All have turned away from God—*Psalm 14:3.*
Minds full of darkness—*Romans 1:21;*
    Ephesians 4:18.
No fear of God—*Romans 3:18.*
Refusal to acknowledge God—*Romans 1:28.*

God's Ministry of Preservation

In Him all things hold together—*Colossians 1:17*.
In Him we live and move and exist—*Acts 17:28*.
Upholds all things by His word—*Hebrews 1:3*.

God's Providential Control

Controls governments—*Romans 13:1*.
Controls kings—*Proverbs 21:1*.
Controls nations—*Psalm 22:28*.
Controls one before birth—*Psalm 139:15,16*.
Makes all things work for good—*Romans 8:28*.

God's Sovereign Decree (Plan)

Declares end from beginning—*Isaiah 46:10*.
Plan includes God's final victory—*1 Corinthians 15:23-28*.
Works out His sovereign purpose—*Ephesians 1:11*.

Golden Rule

Do for others as you would like them to do for
you—*Matthew 7:12; Luke 6:31*.
Love your neighbor as yourself—*Leviticus 19:18*.

Gospel

Good News about Christ—*Romans 1:16*.
Good News about God's kindness—*Acts 20:24*.
Gospel defined—*1 Corinthians 15:1-3*.

Gossip

Do not spread slanderous gossip—*Leviticus 19:16*.
Gossiper betrays confidence—*Proverbs 11:13*.
Gossiper separates close friends—*Proverbs 16:28*.
Gossiper tells secrets—*Proverbs 20:19*.
Gossiping tongue causes anger—*Proverbs 25:23*.

GOVERNMENT

Corrupt government—*Psalm 94:20*.
God controls governments—*Romans 13:1*.
Obey God *over* government—*Acts 5:29*.
Obey the government—*Romans 13:1,5; Titus 3:1*.
Righteous government—*Proverbs 14:34*.
World government coming—*Revelation 13:7*.

GREED

Always greedy for more—*Proverbs 21:26*.
Do not be greedy for money—*1 Peter 5:2*.
Do not be greedy—*Luke 12:15*.
God angry at greed—*Isaiah 57:17*.
Greed harms others—*Psalm 52:7*.
Greedy person tries to get rich quick—*Proverbs 28:22*.
Selfish greed—*Jeremiah 22:17*.

GRIEF

Christ a man of grief—*Isaiah 53:3-10*.
Don't grieve Holy Spirit—*Ephesians 4:30*.
Foolish child brings grief to mother—*Proverbs 10:1*.
Grief of unbelievers—*1 Thessalonians 4:13*.

GROWING SPIRITUALLY

Be rooted in Christ—*Ephesians 3:17-19*.
Grow in grace—*2 Peter 3:18*.
Grow on milk of God's Word—*1 Peter 2:2*.
Let Word of Christ dwell in you—*Colossians 3:16*.
Meditate on things of God—*1 Timothy 4:15*.

GUIDANCE

God guides our feet—*Luke 1:79*.

God will direct your path—*Isaiah 30:21*.
God will show the way to go—*Psalm 32:8*.
God's Spirit guides us—*John 16:13*.
God's Word a lamp—*Psalm 119:105*.

GUILT

Be cleansed of guilty conscience—*Hebrews 10:22*.
Confession cleanses guilt away—*Psalm 51:2*.
Guilt removed—*Psalm 32:5*.
Guilty faces—*Isaiah 3:9*.

HABIT

Habitual cursing—*Psalm 109:17-19*.

Habitual disobedience—*Jeremiah 22:21*.

Habitual hospitality—*Romans 12:13*.

Habitual iniquity—*Micah 2:1*.

Habitual sin—*1 John 3:7-9*.

HALLELUJAH

Hallelujah—*Revelation 19:1*.

Praise the Lord—*Psalm 106:1; 111:1; 112:1; 113:1*.

HAPPINESS

Be happy and do good—*Ecclesiastes 3:12*.

Be happy when times are good—*Ecclesiastes 7:14*.

Forgiveness makes happy—*Psalm 32:1,2*.

Generous man is happy—*Proverbs 22:9*.

Happy are those who avoid wicked—*Psalm 1:1*.

Happy are those who take refuge in God—*Psalm 34:8*.

Happy heart makes face cheerful—*Proverbs 15:13*.

Jesus' formula for happiness—*Matthew 5:3-12*.

Those who trust Lord are happy—*Psalm 84:12*.

HARLOT

Do not let daughter become—*Leviticus 19:29*.

Do not let your heart stray—*Proverbs 7:25,26*.

Wisdom will save you —*Proverbs 2:16*.

HARMONY

Can two walk together without agreeing?—*Amos 3:3*.

Live in harmony and peace—*Psalm 133:1*.

Maintain unity—*John 17:21.*

No harmony between light and darkness—*2 Corinthians 6:14,15.*

HARP

Harps in heaven—*Revelation 5:8; 14:2.*

Praise God with harp—*Psalm 43:4; 71:22; 98:5; 144:9.*

Prayer accompanied by harp—*Habakkuk 3:19.*

Psalm accompanied by harp—*Psalm 4:1; 6:1; 55:1.*

HEALING, GOD DOES NOT ALWAYS GRANT

Epaphroditus near death—*Philippians 2:25-27.*

Paul had "thorn in the flesh"—*2 Corinthians 12:7-9.*

Timothy had stomach problem—*1 Timothy 5:23.*

HEALTH

Gentle words bring life and health—*Proverbs 15:4.*

Jesus healed blind, lame, lepers—*Matthew 15:30; Luke 7:21,22.*

Obedience brings health—*Exodus 15:26.*

Prayer for health—*Isaiah 38:16.*

Restored health for Job—*Job 33:25.*

Satan assaulted Job's health—*Job 2:3-6.*

HEART

Affections of

Avoid lustful desires—*2 Peter 2:10.*

Burning hearts for Jesus—*Luke 24:32.*

Desire for God—*Psalm 73:25.*

Let heaven fill thoughts—*Colossians 3:1,2.*

Love God more than parents—*Matthew 10:37.*

Love God with whole heart—*Deuteronomy 6:5.*
Return to your first love—*Revelation 2:4.*

Known to God

Examines motives—*Proverbs 16:2; Jeremiah 17:10.*
Knows every heart—*1 Kings 8:39; Jeremiah 12:3.*
Knows every plan and thought—*1 Chronicles 28:9.*
Knows everything about us—*Psalm 139:1.*
Knows secrets of every heart—*Psalm 44:21.*
Looks at thoughts and intentions—*1 Samuel 16:7.*

Of Unregenerate People

Fickle hearts—*Hosea 10:2.*
Hard hearts that do not believe—*Ezekiel 2:4.*
Heart deceitful and desperately wicked—*Jeremiah 17:9.*
Heart of pride—*Daniel 5:20.*
Heart that plots evil—*Psalm 140:2; Proverbs 6:14,18.*
Heart that turns away from God—*Hebrews 3:10.*
Stubborn and rebellious hearts—*Jeremiah 5:23.*
Twisted hearts—*Proverbs 11:20.*
Unfaithful hearts and lustful eyes—*Ezekiel 6:9.*

Renewed

Christ can make heart strong—*1 Thessalonians 3:13.*
God can create a clean heart—*Psalm 51:10.* ·
God can give a new heart—*Ezekiel 36:26.*
Lord can cleanse heart—*Deuteronomy 30:6.*

HEATHEN

Babble to false gods—*Matthew 6:7.*
Conspire against God—*Psalm 2:1.*
Detestable—*Leviticus 18:24-30.*
Do not imitate their ways—*Jeremiah 10:2.*

Evil practices—*2 Kings 17:8.*
Idolatrous—*Psalm 135:15.*
Punished by God—*Psalm 44:2; Joel 3:11-13.*
Reap judgment—*Psalm 9:15.*
Scoff at believers—*Psalm 79:10.*
Unclean practices—*Ezra 6:21.*

HEAVEN

Blessing of heaven—*Revelation 22:1-5.*
God's throne—*Isaiah 66:1; Acts 7:49.*
Heavenly homeland—*Hebrews 11:16.*
Holy city—*Revelation 21:1,2.*
Home of righteousness—*2 Peter 3:13.*
Inconceivably wonderful—*1 Corinthians 2:9.*
Jesus preparing place for us—*John 14:1-3.*
New heaven and new earth—*2 Peter 3:13.*
Paradise of God—*2 Corinthians 12:2-4.*

HEDONISM

Constant partying—*Isaiah 5:11,12.*
Godless living—*1 Peter 4:3.*
God's message crowded out by pleasures—*Luke 8:14.*
Love pleasure rather than God—*2 Timothy 3:4.*
Sin nature craves pleasures—*Galatians 5:19-21.*
Slaves to evil pleasures—*Titus 3:3.*
Turn from sinful pleasures—*Titus 2:12.*
Unfaithful hearts and lustful eyes—*Ezekiel 6:9.*

HELL

Eternal punishment—*Matthew 25:46.*
Lake of Fire—*Revelation 20:13-15.*

Place of fire—*Matthew 25:41*.
Place of gloomy dungeons—*2 Peter 2:4*.
Place of torment—*Luke 16:23*.

HELP FROM GOD

Angel of Lord encamps around those who fear Him—*Psalm 34:7*.
Cast all anxiety on God—*1 Peter 5:7*.
Cast burdens on Lord—*Psalm 55:22*.
God will never forsake you—*Hebrews 13:5,6*.
Lord helps those who follow Him—*2 Chronicles 16:9*.
Lord upholds us—*Psalm 37:24*.
No weapon against you will prosper—*Isaiah 54:17*.

HEREDITY

Born blind because of parents?—*John 9:2*.
Descendants of Abraham—*Matthew 3:9*.
Everything reproduces after its kind—*Genesis 1:21,25*.
Flesh gives birth to flesh—*John 3:6*.
Sin inherited from Adam—*Romans 5:12*.

HERESY

Destructive heresies—*2 Peter 2:1*.
Different Jesus, different Spirit—*2 Corinthians 11:4*.
False gospel—*Galatians 1:6-8*.
Upsetting teachings—*Acts 15:24*.

HOLINESS

Be blameless—*Deuteronomy 18:13; Philippians 2:14,15*.
Be holy because God is holy—*Leviticus 11:45; 19:2*.
Be holy in all you do—*Leviticus 20:7; Ephesians 1:4*.
Do not let sin reign in body—*Romans 6:12-14*.

Get rid of all the filth—*James 1:21*.

God blesses those whose hearts are pure—*Matthew 5:8*.

Keep yourself pure—*1 Timothy 5:22; 1 John 3:3*.

Put to death sinful things—*Colossians 3:5*.

Turn from evil, do good—*Psalm 37:27*.

Without holiness one cannot see God—*Hebrews 12:14*.

HOLY SPIRIT

Body is temple of Holy Spirit—*1 Corinthians 6:19*.

Comforter—*John 14:16; 15:26; 16:7*.

Day of Pentecost—*Acts 2*.

Descended on Jesus like dove—*Matthew 3:16*.

Do not grieve Holy Spirit—*Ephesians 4:30*.

Do not quench Holy Spirit—*1 Thessalonians 5:19*.

Fruit of the Spirit—*Galatians 5:22,23*.

God pours out Spirit on all people—*Ezekiel 39:29*.

Joy from the Holy Spirit—*Romans 14:17*.

Power of the Holy Spirit—*Romans 15:13*.

Promise of power from Spirit—*Acts 1:8*.

Renewed by the Holy Spirit—*Titus 3:5*.

Spirit reminds us of Jesus' teachings—*John 14:26*.

Walk in dependence on Spirit—*Galatians 6:8*.

Activities of

Baptizes believers—*1 Corinthians 12:13*.

Convicts of sin—*John 16:8-11*.

Fills believers—*Ephesians 5:18*.

Gives spiritual gifts—*Romans 12:6-8*.

Illumines God's Word for us—
1 Corinthians 2:9–3:2.

Indwells believers—*1 Corinthians 6:19*.

Inspired Scripture—*2 Peter 1:21*.

Prays for us—*Romans 8:26*.

Produces fruit in us—*Galatians 5:22,23*.

Regenerates believers—*Titus 3:5*.

Restrains sin—*Genesis 6:3*.

Seals believers unto day of redemption—
Ephesians 4:30.

Teaches believers—*John 16:12-15*.

Testifies of Christ—*John 15:26*.

Deity of

Holy Spirit is eternal—*Hebrews 9:14*.

Inspired Scripture—*2 Peter 1:21*.

Is called the Spirit of God—*1 Corinthians 6:11*.

Is one person in the divine Trinity—*Matthew 28:19*.

Lying to Holy Spirit is lying to God—*Acts 5:3,4*.

Omnipresent—*Psalm 139:7-10*.

Omniscient—*1 Corinthians 2:11*.

Personhood of

Can be lied to like a person—*Acts 5:3*.

Can be obeyed like a person—*Acts 10:19-21*.

Can be outraged like a person—*Hebrews 10:29*.

Commands like a person—*Acts 13:2*.

Has emotion—*Ephesians 4:30*.

Has intelligence—*1 Corinthians 2:10,11*.

Personal pronouns used of Him—*John 15:26*.

Prays like a person—*Romans 8:26*.

Teaches like a person—*Luke 12:11,12; John 14:26*.

Testifies like a person—*John 15:26*.

HOMICIDE

Accidental

Cities of refuge, flee to—*Exodus 21:13; Numbers 35:11.*
Unintentional killing—*Deuteronomy 19:4-7.*

Murder

Commandment not to murder—*Exodus 20:13.*
From the heart comes murder—*Matthew 15:19.*
Lord detests murderers—*Psalm 5:6.*
Murder is forbidden—*Genesis 9:5.*

HOMOSEXUAL

Do not practice homosexuality—*Genesis 19:5-7.*
Homosexuals have no share in Kingdom—*1 Corinthians 6:9.*
Penalty for homosexual acts—*Leviticus 20:13.*

HONESTY

Be honorable before Lord—*2 Corinthians 8:21.*
God likes integrity—*1 Chronicles 29:17.*
Golden Rule—*Matthew 7:12; Luke 6:31.*
Honest answers are appreciated—*Proverbs 24:26.*
Lord delights in honesty—*Proverbs 11:1.*
Lord demands fairness—*Proverbs 16:11.*
Lord despises double standards—*Proverbs 20:10,23.*

HONOR

Fear of Lord brings honor and life—*Proverbs 22:4.*
God blesses with riches, honor—*2 Chronicles 1:12.*
Honor father and mother—*Exodus 20:12.*
Honor God with thanksgiving—*Psalm 69:30.*

Humble will be honored—*Proverbs 15:33; 18:12; 29:23.*

Husbands give honor to wives—*1 Peter 3:7.*

Jesus given highest place of honor—*Hebrews 7:26.*

Wisdom and virtue lead to honor—*Proverbs 3:16.*

HOPE

Be strong and take courage—*Psalm 31:24.*

Confident assurance—*Hebrews 11:1.*

Everlasting comfort and hope—*2 Thessalonians 2:16.*

Faith and hope in God—*1 Peter 1:21.*

Hope deferred makes heart sick—*Proverbs 13:12.*

Hope gives endurance—*1 Thessalonians 1:3.*

Hope in God—*Psalm 39:7; 43:5; 71:5.*

Hope in God's Word—*Psalm 119:74,81; 130:5.*

Those who hope in Lord renew strength—
Isaiah 40:31.

Three endure: faith, hope, love—*1 Corinthians 13:13.*

We have a living hope—*1 Peter 1:3.*

HOSPITALITY

Feed and give water to brothers—*Matthew 25:31-46.*

Golden Rule—*Matthew 7:12; Luke 6:31.*

Show hospitality to strangers—*Hebrews 13:2.*

HUMAN BEINGS, EQUALITY OF

From one man God created all the nations—*Acts 17:26.*

Never think of anyone as impure—*Acts 10:28.*

No Jew/Gentile, slave/free, male/female in Christ—
Galatians 3:28.

HUMILITY

Be clothed with humility—*Colossians 3:12; 1 Peter 5:5,6.*

Be compassionate and humble—*1 Peter 3:8.*
Be humble and gentle—*Ephesians 4:2.*
Consider others as better—*Philippians 2:3.*
Do not praise yourself; let others do it—*Proverbs 27:2.*
God gives grace to the humble—*Proverbs 3:34.*
God guides the humble—*Psalm 25:9.*
God prospers the humble—*Job 5:11.*
Humble will be exalted—*Matthew 23:12.*
Humble will be filled with fresh joy—*Isaiah 29:19.*
Humble will be honored—*Proverbs 15:33; 18:12; 29:23.*
Humility brings healing—*2 Chronicles 7:14.*
Lord supports the humble—*Psalm 147:6.*
Walk humbly with your God—*Micah 6:8.*

HUNGER

Feed brothers—*Matthew 25:31-46.*
Feed hungry enemies—*Romans 12:20.*
Hunger for righteousness—*Matthew 5:6.*
Jesus fed hungry thousands—*Mark 6:30-44.*
No more hunger in heaven—*Revelation 7:16.*

HUSBAND

Do not deprive wife sexually—*1 Corinthians 7:3-5.*
Give honor to wives—*1 Peter 3:7.*
Live happily with woman you love—*Ecclesiastes 9:9.*
Love your wives—*Colossians 3:19.*
Share your love only with your wife—*Proverbs 5:15.*
Two become one flesh—*Matthew 19:5; Mark 10:7.*
Wives should submit to—*Ephesians 5:22.*

HYPOCRISY

Be done with hypocrisy—*1 Peter 2:1.*
Do not fast like hypocrites do—*Matthew 6:16.*
Do not pray like hypocrites do—*Matthew 6:5.*
Get rid of log from your own eye—*Matthew 7:5.*
Hypocrites filthy on inside—*Luke 11:39; 16:15.*

IDLENESS

Full of excuses—*Proverbs 22:13; 26:13.*

Hands refuse to work—*Proverbs 21:25; Ecclesiastes 4:5.*

Lazy people a pain to their employer—*Proverbs 10:26.*

Lazy people soon poor—*Proverbs 10:4; 14:23.*

Love of sleep—*Proverbs 20:13.*

On the road to poverty—*Proverbs 23:21.*

Take a lesson from the ants—*Proverbs 6:6.*

Whoever does not work should not eat—*2 Thessalonians 3:10.*

IDOL

Destroy idols—*Genesis 35:2.*

Do not corrupt yourselves—*Deuteronomy 4:25.*

Do not make idols—*Exodus 20:4; Leviticus 26:1.*

Do not turn to idols—*Leviticus 19:4.*

Do not worship other gods—*Deuteronomy 5:7.*

Flee from worship of idols—*1 Corinthians 10:14.*

Golden calf—*Exodus 32:4.*

Idols detestable to the Lord—*Deuteronomy 27:15.*

Make no gods for yourselves—*Exodus 34:17.*

IDOLATRY, WICKED PRACTICES OF

Child sacrifices—*Leviticus 18:21; 20:2; 2 Kings 3:27.*

Detestable acts—*Deuteronomy 12:31.*

Pagan revelry—*1 Corinthians 10:7.*

Shrine prostitutes—*1 Kings 14:24; 15:12.*

Sorcery and divination—*2 Kings 21:6.*

IGNORANCE

Ignorance of true God—*Acts 17:23*.
Lean not on own understanding—*Proverbs 3:5,6*.
Now we see imperfectly—*1 Corinthians 13:9,12*.
Zeal without knowledge is not good—*Proverbs 19:2*.

IMAGINATION

Consistently evil thoughts—*Genesis 6:5*.
Fix thoughts on what is true—*Philippians 4:8*.
Foolish ideas—*Romans 1:21*.
Let heaven fill thoughts—*Colossians 3:1,2*.
Lust in one's thoughts—*Matthew 5:28*.
Myths—*1 Timothy 1:4; 2 Timothy 4:4; Titus 1:14*.
Old wives' tales—*1 Timothy 4:7*.

IMITATING JESUS

Be humble like Jesus—*Philippians 2:3-8*.
Be transformed—*2 Corinthians 3:18*.
Follow Jesus' lead—*John 13:12-15*.
Love like Jesus—*John 13:34,35*.
Obey like Jesus—*John 15:9-11*.
Paul imitated Christ—*1 Corinthians 11:1*.
Walk as Jesus walked—*1 John 2:6*.

IMMATURITY

Infants in Christ—*1 Corinthians 3:1,2*.
Leave immaturity behind—*Proverbs 9:6*.
No longer infants—*Ephesians 4:14*.
Stop thinking like children—*1 Corinthians 14:20*.
You need milk, not solid food—*Hebrews 5:12,13*.

IMMORALITY

Immoral lives—*Jude 4.*

No immoral living—*Romans 13:13.*

Playing with fire—*Proverbs 6:27.*

Repent of sexual immorality—*2 Corinthians 12:21.*

Run from immoral woman—*Proverbs 5:8.*

Satan tempts believers—*1 Corinthians 7:5.*

Watch out for immoral women—*Proverbs 2:16; 5:3.*

IMMORTALITY

Better things waiting for us in eternity—*Hebrews 10:34.*

Free gift of God is eternal life—*Matthew 25:46.*

Hold tightly to eternal life—*1 Timothy 6:12.*

Jesus gives us eternal life—*John 10:28.*

Jesus is the resurrection and the life—*John 11:25,26.*

IMPARTIALITY OF GOD

Does not tolerate partiality—*Deuteronomy 10:17.*

Has no favorites—*Romans 2:11; Ephesians 6:9.*

IMPENITENCE

Blind and stubborn—*Psalm 81:11,12.*

Deaf to truth—*Acts 7:51.*

Do not harden your hearts—*Hebrews 3:8.*

Growing increasingly bold in wickedness—*Psalm 52:7.*

No remorse—*Jeremiah 44:10.*

Rebellion is as bad as witchcraft—*1 Samuel 15:23.*

Refusal to obey—*Psalm 106:25.*

INCARNATION, NECESSITY OF CHRIST'S

Came as sacrifice for sin—*Hebrews 10:1-10.*

Came to become our High Priest—*Hebrews 5:1,2.*
Came to destroy works of devil—*1 John 3:8.*
Came to fulfill Davidic Covenant—*Luke 1:31-33.*
Came to give an example for living—*1 Peter 2:21.*
Came to reveal God—*John 1:18.*

INCONSISTENCY

Get log out of your own eye—*Matthew 7:3.*
Scribes and Pharisees—*Matthew 23:3,4.*

INDECISION

Hearts of people are fickle—*Hosea 10:2.*
No one can serve two masters—*Matthew 6:24.*
Waver back and forth—*1 Kings 18:21; James 1:8.*

INDUSTRY

Hard work means prosperity—*Proverbs 12:11.*
Hard workers get rich—*Proverbs 10:4.*
Hard workers have plenty of food—*Proverbs 28:19.*
Never be lazy in your work—*Romans 12:11.*
Wealth from hard work grows—*Proverbs 13:11.*
Whatever you do, do well—*Ecclesiastes 9:10.*
Work brings profit—*Proverbs 14:23.*
Work hard and become a leader—*Proverbs 12:24.*

INFLUENCE

Be example to other Christians—*1 Thessalonians 1:7.*
Influence spouse—*1 Corinthians 7:16.*
Influence unbelieving neighbors—*1 Peter 2:12.*
Let your light shine—*Mark 4:21; Luke 11:33.*

INHERITANCE, SPIRITUAL

Inheritance from God—*Ephesians 1:11.*

Inheritance of Christ's treasures—*Romans 8:17*.
Inheritance of eternal life—*Titus 3:7*.

INJUSTICE

Do not exploit widows or orphans—*Exodus 22:22*.
Do not falsely charge anyone—*Exodus 23:7*.
Do not pass along false reports—*Exodus 23:1*.
Do not twist justice—*Exodus 23:6*.

INSENSITIVE

Hardening of hearts—*Psalm 95:8*.
Seared conscience—*1 Timothy 4:1,2*.
Unconcerned about right and wrong—*Ephesians 4:19*.
Unconcerned for God or man—*Luke 18:1-5*.

INSTABILITY

Doubtful mind is unsettled—*James 1:6*.
Failure to love Christ as at first—*Revelation 2:4*.
Fickle hearts—*Hosea 10:2*.
Galatians turned from gospel of grace—*Galatians 1:6*.
Neither hot nor cold—*Revelation 3:15,16*.
No one can serve two masters—*Matthew 6:24*.

INSTRUCTION OF CHILDREN

Bring children up with discipline—*Ephesians 6:4*.
Teach children about God—*Exodus 10:2*.
Teach children to choose right path—*Proverbs 22:6*.

INTEGRITY

Fix thoughts on what is right—*Philippians 4:8*.
Godly walk with integrity—*Proverbs 20:7*.
Live by Golden Rule—*Luke 6:31*.

INTERCESSION OF MAN WITH GOD

Elders pray over the sick—*James 5:14*.
Pray for all people—*1 Timothy 2:1,2*.
Pray for Christians everywhere—*Ephesians 6:18*.

INTOXICATION

Be filled with Spirit, not drunk—*Ephesians 5:18*.
Brings affliction—*Proverbs 23:29,30*.
Leads to brawls—*Proverbs 20:1*.
Leads to shame—*Joel 1:5; Psalm 69:12*.
Robs people of clear thinking—*Hosea 4:11*.

JEALOUSY

Arouses husband's fury—*Proverbs 6:34*.

Destructive nature—*Proverbs 27:4*.

Mark of the flesh—*Galatians 5:19,20*.

JESUS CHRIST

Ascension of

Ascension to Father—*John 7:33; 16:28; 20:17*.

Jesus going to prepare a place—*John 14:2*.

Jesus told disciples He was going away—*John 14:12,28*.

Taken up into heaven—*Mark 16:19; Luke 24:51*.

Taken up into the sky—*Acts 1:9*.

Compassion of

Compassion for peoples' hunger—*Matthew 15:32*.

Compassion for people without shepherd—*Mark 6:34*.

Had compassion and healed the sick—*Matthew 14:14*.

Creator

Created everything—*John 1:3; Colossians 1:16*.

Universe made through Jesus—*1 Corinthians 8:6*.

World made through Jesus—*John 1:10*.

Death of

Atoning sacrifice—*1 John 2:2*.

Betrayed, flogged, killed, and raised—*Matthew 17:22,23*.

Bore our sins in His body—*1 Peter 2:24*.

Gave His life as ransom—*Mark 10:45; 1 Timothy 2:5,6*.

Good Shepherd laid down life—*John 10:11-18*.

Lamb who was killed—*Isaiah 53:7; Revelation 5:12.*
Pierced hands and feet—*Psalm 22:16; Zechariah 12:10.*
Purchased salvation by blood—*Revelation 5:9.*

Deity of
Alpha and Omega—*Revelation 1:8; 22:13,16.*
Elohim, Mighty God—*Isaiah 9:6.*
Equated with the "I AM" of Exodus 3:14—*John 8:58.*
Father addressed Jesus as God—*Hebrews 1:8.*
First and the Last—*Revelation 1:17.*
Forgives sins (which only God can do)—*Mark 2:5-12.*
Fullness of deity lives in bodily form—*Colossians 2:9.*
God the One and Only—*John 1:18.*
Great God and Savior—*Titus 2:13.*
Has nature of God—*Philippians 2:6.*
Image of the invisible God—*Colossians 1:15.*
Immanuel, God with us—*Matthew 1:23.*
Is God—*John 1:1.*
King of kings and Lord of lords—*Revelation 19:16.*
Omnipresent—*Matthew 28:20; Ephesians 1:22,23.*
Omniscient—*Revelation 2–3.*
Sustains universe as God—*Colossians 1:17.*
Thomas called Jesus God—*John 20:28.*
Worshipped as God—*Matthew 28:16,17; Hebrews 1:6.*

Eternity of
Everlasting Father—*Isaiah 9:6.*
Existed before Abraham—*John 8:58.*
Existed before everything else began—*Colossians 1:17.*
Existed from the beginning—*1 John 1:1.*

First and the Last—*Revelation 1:17.*

Is, was, and is still to come—*Revelation 1:8.*

Exaltation of

Ascended higher than all the heavens—*Ephesians 4:10.*

Crowned with glory and honor—*Hebrews 2:9.*

Exalted to God's right hand—*Luke 22:69; Acts 2:33,34.*

Name above every other name—*Philippians 2:9.*

Holiness of

Born as holy babe—*Luke 1:35.*

Holy and blameless—*Hebrews 7:26.*

Holy, righteous one—*Acts 3:14.*

Holy servant—*Acts 4:27,30.*

Never sinned—*2 Corinthians 5:21; Hebrews 4:15.*

Sinless, spotless Lamb of God—*1 Peter 1:19.*

Humanity of in the Incarnation

Became flesh—*John 1:14; Hebrews 2:14,17,18.*

Became human—*John 1:14.*

Born of a virgin—*Isaiah 7:14.*

Born of a woman—*Genesis 3:15; Galatians 4:4.*

Called a man—*1 Timothy 2:5.*

Flesh and bones body—*Luke 24:39.*

Had a human nature—*Romans 1:2,3.*

Took on human appearance—*Philippians 2:7.*

Humility of

He is humble—*Matthew 21:5.*

Led as a sheep to the slaughter—*Acts 8:32.*

Made Himself nothing—*Philippians 2:7.*

Washed disciples' feet—*John 13:5.*

Judge

Great Judge is coming—*James 5:9*.
Judge of all—*Acts 10:42*.
We must all stand before Christ—*2 Corinthians 5:10*.
Will judge the world—*Acts 17:31*.

King

Government will rest on His shoulders—*Isaiah 9:6*.
Heir to David's throne—*Isaiah 11:10; Acts 2:30*.
King is coming—*John 12:15*.
King of kings—*1 Timothy 6:15; Revelation 17:14; 19:16*.
Kingship—*John 18:37*.

Lord

Christ the Lord—*Luke 2:11*.
Confess that Jesus is Lord—*Romans 10:9*.
Do all in name of the Lord—*Colossians 3:17,23,24*.
Every knee will bow before—*Philippians 2:9-11*.
In your heart, set apart Jesus as Lord—*1 Peter 3:15*.
Lord of lords—*Revelation 17:14*.
One Lord—*1 Corinthians 8:6*.
We preach Jesus as Lord—*2 Corinthians 4:5*.

Love of

Compassion—*Matthew 9:36; 14:14; 15:32; Luke 7:13*.
Died for us—*Matthew 8:17; John 10:11; 1 John 3:16*.
Full of love—*2 Corinthians 8:9*.

Meekness of

Gentle and kind—*2 Corinthians 10:1*.
Humble—*Matthew 21:5*.
Humble position of servant—*Philippians 2:7,8*.

Miracles of

Blind see, lame walk, deaf hear—*Matthew 15:30.*
Healed diseases—*Matthew 4:23,24; 14:14; Luke 4:40.*
Miraculous fish catching—*John 21:6.*
Miraculous signs—*John 2:23; 3:2.*
Turned water into wine—*John 4:46.*

Mission of

Appointed to preach Good News—*Luke 4:18.*
Came to die for sinners—*Romans 5:6.*
Came to give life as ransom—*Matthew 20:28.*
Came to save His people from sins—*Matthew 1:21.*

Names and Titles of

Alpha and Omega—*Revelation 1:8; 22:13.*
Bread of Life—*John 6:48.*
Eternal High Priest—*Hebrews 6:20.*
Faithful and True—*Revelation 19:11.*
First and the Last—*Revelation 1:17.*
God and Savior—*2 Peter 1:1.*
Good Shepherd—*John 10:11.*
Great God and Savior—*Titus 2:13.*
Great High Priest—*Hebrews 4:14.*
Great Shepherd—*Hebrews 13:20.*
Immanuel—*Isaiah 7:14; Matthew 1:23.*
King of kings and Lord of lords—*Revelation 19:16.*
Lamb of God—*John 1:29.*
Last Adam—*1 Corinthians 15:45.*
Light of the world—*John 8:12.*
Lord—*Mark 1:2,3; Acts 2:21.*
Lord and Savior—*2 Peter 1:11.*

Lord over lords and King over kings—*Revelation 17:14*.
Mediator—*1 Timothy 2:5*.
Messiah—*Matthew 1:1; 16:20; Luke 9:20; 23:2*.
Mighty God—*Isaiah 9:6*.
Mighty Savior—*Luke 1:69*.
Prophet—*Deuteronomy 18:15,18; Matthew 21:11*.
Righteous One—*Acts 7:52; 22:14*.
Savior—*Luke 2:11,30; Titus 1:4; 1 John 4:14*.
Shepherd—*Mark 14:27*.
Son of God—*Matthew 26:63-65; Luke 1:35; John 1:49*.
Son of Man—*Mark 2:28*.
True light—*John 1:9*.
True vine—*John 15:1*.
Way, truth, and life—*John 14:6*.
Wonderful Counselor, Mighty God—*Isaiah 9:6*.
Word—*John 1:1; Revelation 19:13*.

Obedience of

Came to do Father's will—*Matthew 26:39,42*.
Does exactly what Father commands—*John 14:30,31*.
Obedient to death—*Philippians 2:8*.
Totally obedient—*Romans 5:18,19*.

X Omnipotence of

➤ Cast out evil spirits, healed disease—*Matthew 10:1*.
Mighty God—*Isaiah 9:6*.
Opens doors no one can shut—*Revelation 3:7*.
Raised people from the dead—*John 11:1-44*.
Sustains universe by mighty power—*Colossians 1:17*.
Wind and waves obey Him—*Matthew 8:27*.

Omnipresence of

Fills everything with His presence—*Ephesians 1:23*.
Jesus is with us always—*Matthew 28:20*.
Where two or three are—*Matthew 18:20*.

Omniscience of

Knew Nathanael's situation from afar—*John 1:48*.
Knew who would betray Him—*John 13:11*.
Knows everything—*John 16:30; 21:17*.
Knows Father as Father knows Him—*Matthew 11:27*.
Knows motives—*Matthew 22:18*.
Knows thoughts—*Matthew 12:25; Luke 6:8*.
Searches intentions of every person—*Revelation 2:23*.

Preaching and Teaching

Olivet Discourse—*Matthew 24–25*.
Sermon on the Mount—*Matthew 5–7*.
Upper Room Discourse—*John 14–16*.

Preexistence

Before Abraham, "I am"—*John 8:58*.
Existed before creation—*Colossians 1:15*.
Existed before the beginning—*John 1:1*.

Present Activities of

Answers our prayers—*John 14:13,14*.
Builds the church—*Matthew 16:18*.
Head of the church—*Ephesians 1:20-23*.
Helps us bear fruit—*John 15:1-10*.
Intercedes for us—*John 17:15; Hebrews 7:25; 1 John 2:1*.
Preparing an eternal abode for us—*John 14:1-3*.
Sympathetic High Priest—*Hebrews 4:15*.

Priesthood

Eternal High Priest—*Hebrews 6:20.*

Great High Priest—*Hebrews 4:14,15.*

High Priest with superior ministry—*Hebrews 8:6.*

Priest forever in line of Melchizedek—*Hebrews 5:6.*

Prophecies of

Betrayed for 30 pieces of silver—*Zechariah 11:12,13.*

Born from line of David—*2 Samuel 7:12,13.*

Born in Bethlehem—*Micah 5:2.*

Born of a virgin—*Isaiah 7:14.*

Born of seed of a woman—*Genesis 3:15.*

Born of seed of Abraham—*Genesis 12:1-3.*

Crucified—*Zechariah 12:10.*

Disciples scattered after crucifixion—*Zechariah 13:7.*

Mocked and shamed—*Psalm 69:7; 109:25.*

Resurrected—*Psalm 16:10.*

Slain for our iniquities—*Isaiah 53:3-7.*

Relation to Father

Came from the Father—*John 16:28.*

Came to do Father's will—*John 6:38; 14:31.*

Does what Father does—*John 5:19.*

Existed with Father in beginning—*John 1:1,2.*

Father and Jesus are one—*John 10:30.*

Father draws people to Jesus—*John 6:44.*

Father is "greater" positionally—*John 14:28.*

Jesus honors the Father—*John 8:49.*

Jesus knows the Father—*John 10:15.*

Jesus obeys the Father—*John 15:10.*

Jesus prayed to Father—*Matthew 26:39.*

Jesus sits at Father's right hand—*Acts 2:33*.
Jesus speaks message of Father—*John 7:16; 8:28; 12:50*.
Jesus was sent into world by Father—*John 3:34; 4:34*.
Jesus will turn kingdom to Father—*1 Corinthians 15:24*.

Resurrection

Alive forever and ever—*Revelation 1:18*.
Angel announced, He is risen—*Matthew 28:6,7*.
Appeared for 40 days—*Acts 1:3*.
Christ's resurrection, gospel—*1 Corinthians 15:1-4*.
First to rise from the dead—*Revelation 1:5*.
Firstfruits of resurrection—*Colossians 1:18*.
Flesh and bones body—*Luke 24:39*.
If Christ not raised, faith vain—*1 Corinthians 15:17,20*.
Jesus raised Himself—*John 2:19-22*.
Prophecy, body won't rot in grave—*Psalm 16:10*.
Sign of the prophet Jonah—*Matthew 16:4*.
Will never die again—*Romans 6:9*.

Savior

Birth of the Savior—*Luke 2:11*.
Came into world to save sinners—*1 Timothy 1:15*.
Came to seek and save the lost—*Luke 19:10*.
God's promised Savior—*Acts 13:23*.
Great God and Savior—*Titus 2:13*.
Jesus will save His people—*Matthew 1:21*.
Salvation in no one else—*Acts 4:12*.
Savior—*Ephesians 5:23; Philippians 3:20*.
Savior has appeared—*2 Timothy 1:10*.
Savior of all men—*1 Timothy 4:10*.
Savior of the world—*John 4:42; 1 John 4:14*.

Sinlessness

Committed no sin—*2 Corinthians 5:21; 1 Peter 2:22,23*.
Holy One—*Luke 1:35*.
In Him is no sin—*1 John 3:4,5*.
Lamb without blemish—*1 Peter 1:18,19*.
Unblemished—*Hebrews 9:14*.
Without sin—*Hebrews 4:15*.

Son of God

Authority of Son—*1 Corinthians 15:28*.
Father says, You are my Son—*Psalm 2:7; Hebrews 1:5*.
Father's beloved Son—*Matthew 3:17; 17:5; Mark 1:11*.
Glory of the Son—*John 1:14*.
Sacrifice of the Son—*1 John 4:10*.
Son brings glory to Father—*John 14:13*.
Son can do nothing by Himself—*John 5:19*.
Son has life in Himself—*John 5:26*.
Son of the blessed God—*Mark 14:61*.
Son of the Most High God—*Mark 5:7; Luke 8:28*.

Temptation of

Faced same temptations we do—*Hebrews 4:15*.
Never sinned—*2 Corinthians 5:21; Hebrews 4:15*.
Overcame world—*John 16:33*.
Sinless, spotless Lamb of God—*1 Peter 1:19*.
Tempted by the devil—*Matthew 4:1-11; Mark 1:12,13*.
There is no sin in Him—*1 John 3:5*.

Worship of

Angels worshipped Him—*Hebrews 1:6*.
At name of Jesus every knee bow—*Philippians 2:10*.

Disciples worshipped—*Matthew 14:33.*
Magi worshipped—*Matthew 2:2,11.*

JEWELS

Armbands, bracelets, rings, earrings—*Numbers 31:50.*
Earrings, rings—*Exodus 35:22.*
Jewelry, bracelets—*Ezekiel 16:11,12.*
Silver and gold jewelry—*Genesis 24:53; Exodus 3:22.*

JOY

Cheerful look brings joy—*Proverbs 15:30.*
Comes from abiding in Christ—*John 15:10,11.*
Filled with joy and with the Holy Spirit—*Acts 13:52.*
Fruit of the spirit—*Galatians 5:22.*
Fullness of joy in God's presence—*Psalm 16:11.*
God turns mourning into joy—*Jeremiah 31:13.*
God's commands bring joy to heart—*Psalm 19:8.*
Humble will be filled with fresh joy—*Isaiah 29:19.*
Joy at answered prayer—*John 16:24.*
Joy for those whose rebellion is forgiven—
    Psalm 32:1,2.
Joy from the Holy Spirit—*Romans 14:17.*
Joy in trusting God—*Psalm 40:4.*
Look forward to joys of heaven—*Colossians 1:5.*
Plant in tears, harvest joy—*Psalm 126:5.*
Take joy in doing God's will—*Psalm 40:8.*
Trials, count it all joy—*James 1:2.*

JUDGMENT

After death comes judgment—*Hebrews 9:27.*
Believers judged by Christ—*1 Corinthians 3:10-15.*

Day of judgment coming—*2 Peter 3:7.*
God will judge the good and bad—*Ecclesiastes 3:17.*
Great White Throne judgment—*Revelation 20:12.*
Jesus is judge of all men—*John 5:22; Acts 17:31.*
Judgment awaits all of us—*Matthew 12:36.*
Nations judged at Second Coming—*Joel 3:2.*

JUSTICE

Blessed are those who seek justice—*Psalm 106:3.*
Do not pervert justice—*Leviticus 19:15.*
God loves justice—*Psalm 99:4; Isaiah 61:8.*
God will bring about justice—*Luke 18:7,8.*
God will judge world with justice—*Acts 17:31.*
Good comes to those who seek justice—*Psalm 112:5.*
Jesus will reign in justice—*Isaiah 9:7.*
Justice at the Second Coming—*Revelation 19:11.*
Justice gives a country stability—*Proverbs 29:4.*

JUSTIFICATION

Abram declared righteous—*Genesis 15:6.*
Justified by faith—*Acts 13:39; Romans 3:28; 5:1.*
Justified by God's grace—*Romans 3:23,24.*
Justified in the name of Jesus—*1 Corinthians 6:11.*
Law does not justify—*Romans 3:20.*

KINDNESS

Always be kind—*1 Thessalonians 5:15*.
Be kind and compassionate—*Ephesians 4:32*.
Be kind to everyone—*2 Timothy 2:24*.
Fruit of the spirit includes kindness—*Galatians 5:22*.
Kind words cheer people up—*Proverbs 12:25*.
Kindhearted woman—*Proverbs 11:16*.
Kindness of wife—*Proverbs 31:26*.
Kindness to the poor—*Proverbs 19:17*.
Maintain brotherly kindness—*2 Peter 1:5-7*.
Show mercy and kindness—*Zechariah 7:9*.

KINGDOM OF HEAVEN

Become like children to enter—*Matthew 18:3*.
Hard for rich person to enter—*Matthew 19:23,24*.
Keys of Kingdom of Heaven—*Matthew 16:19*.
Parable of the growing seed—*Mark 4:26-29*.
Parable of the hidden treasure—*Matthew 13:44-46*.
Parable of mustard seed and yeast—*Matthew 13:31-43*.
Parable of the net—*Matthew 13:47-52*.
Parable of the talents—*Matthew 25:14-30*.
Parable of the ten virgins—*Matthew 25:1-13*.
Parable of the wedding banquet—*Matthew 22:1-14*.
Parable of the weeds—*Matthew 13:24-30*.
Parable of workers in the vineyard—*Matthew 20:1-16*.
Parable of unmerciful servant—*Matthew 18:21-35*.
Secrets of the kingdom of God—*Luke 8:10*.

Kiss

Greet each other with holy kiss—*Romans 16:16*.
Judas betrayed Jesus with kiss—*Luke 22:48*.
Wound of friend better than—*Proverbs 27:6*.

Knowledge

Fear of Lord is beginning of knowledge—*Proverbs 1:7*.
Gift of special knowledge—*1 Corinthians 12:8*.
Knowing Christ is priceless—*Philippians 3:8*.
Knowing God, most important—*Hosea 6:6*.
Lord gives understanding—*1 Kings 3:9*.
Lord teaches good judgment—*Psalm 119:66*.
Wise person is hungry for truth—*Proverbs 15:14*.

LABOR

Do not be lazy—*Romans 12:11; 2 Thessalonians 3:7.*
Hard work means prosperity—*Proverbs 10:4; 12:11.*
Whatever you do, do well—*Ecclesiastes 9:10.*
Work brings profit—*Proverbs 14:23.*
Work hard and become a leader—*Proverbs 12:24.*
Work with your hands—*1 Thessalonians 4:11.*

LAKE OF FIRE

Death and Hades thrown in—*Revelation 20:14.*
Devil thrown in—*Revelation 20:10.*
Sinners thrown in—*Revelation 21:8.*
Those not in Book of Life thrown in—*Revelation 20:15.*

LAMB OF GOD

Blood of the Lamb—*Revelation 12:11.*
Lamb takes away sin of the world—*John 1:29.*
Lamb victorious—*Revelation 17:14.*
Lamb's Book—*Revelation 21:27.*
Throne of God and of the Lamb—*Revelation 22:3.*
Wrath of the Lamb—*Revelation 6:16.*

LANGUAGE

Avoid foul or abusive language—*Romans 3:13,14.*
Good words come from good heart—*Matthew 12:35.*
Let your conversation be gracious—*Colossians 4:6.*
Rid mouth of filthy language—*Colossians 3:8.*

LASCIVIOUSNESS

Avoid lustful passions—*1 Thessalonians 4:4,5.*

Body not for sexual immorality—*1 Corinthians 6:13*.
Do not chase evil desires—*1 Peter 4:2,3*.
Have nothing to do with sexual sin—*Colossians 3:5*.
Immoral lives—*Jude 4*.
No immoral living—*Romans 13:13*.
No indulging in sexual sin—*1 Corinthians 6:9*.
Repent of sexual immorality—*2 Corinthians 12:21*.
Run from immoral woman—*Proverbs 5:8*.
Sexual immorality comes from heart—*Mark 7:21*.
Sexual immorality, sinful nature—*Galatians 5:19*.

LAW

Function of

Reveals holiness of God—*Romans 7:12*.
Reveals what sin is—*Romans 7:7*.
Tutor that leads us to Christ—*Galatians 3:24*.

God's

God's law in human hearts—*Romans 2:14,15*.
Jesus came to fulfill law—*Matthew 5:17-20*.
Law is holy—*Romans 7:12*.
Law of Lord revives the soul—*Psalm 19:7*.
Law shows sin—*Romans 7:7*.

Temporary

Christ accomplished purpose of law—*Romans 10:4*.
Jesus ended the law—*Ephesians 2:15*.
Law of Moses was only a shadow—*Hebrews 10:1*.

LAWSUITS

Come to terms quickly with enemy—*Matthew 5:25*.

Do not be in hurry to go to court—*Proverbs 25:8*.
Why file lawsuit against Christian?—*1 Corinthians 6:1*.

LAZINESS

Do not be lazy—*Hebrews 6:12*.
Laziness leads to poverty—*Proverbs 10:4*.
Lazy people, pain to employer—*Proverbs 10:26*.
Lazy people are full of excuses—*Proverbs 22:13; 26:13*.
Lazy people want much but get little—*Proverbs 13:4*.
Never be lazy in your work—*Romans 12:11*.
Sluggard reaps no harvest—*Proverbs 20:4*.
Take a lesson from the ants—*Proverbs 6:6*.
Whoever not work, not eat—*2 Thessalonians 3:10*.

LEADERSHIP

Christ head over all authorities—*Colossians 2:9,10*.
Confidence in leader—*1 Corinthians 3:21*.
Humble leaders—*Exodus 3:11; Judges 6:15; Isaiah 6:5*.
Imitate church leaders—*Hebrews 13:7*.
Importance of prayer by leaders—*Luke 6:12-16*.
Lead gently—*Galatians 6:1,2*.
Leaders lead by good example—*1 Peter 5:3*.
Obey spiritual leaders—*Hebrews 13:17*.
Rebellious leaders—*Isaiah 1:23*.
Respect church leadership—*1 Thessalonians 5:12,13*.
Servant leaders—*Matthew 20:28; Mark 10:43,44*.
Work hard and become a leader—*Proverbs 12:24*.

LEAVEN

Beware the yeast of the Pharisees—*Mark 8:15*.
Kingdom of Heaven is like yeast—*Matthew 13:33*.

Yeast of Pharisees and Sadducees—*Matthew 16:6.*
Yeast spreads quickly—*Galatians 5:9.*

LEGALISM

Breaking the Sabbath—*Mark 2:24; Luke 6:2; 13:14.*
Letter kills, Spirit gives life—*2 Corinthians 3:6.*
No food is unclean in itself—*Romans 14:14.*
Paul previously zealous for law—*Acts 22:3.*
Weighty burden—*Luke 11:45,46.*

LENDING

Be willing to loan to anyone—*Luke 6:34,35.*
Borrower is servant to lender—*Proverbs 22:7.*
Do not charge interest—*Exodus 22:25.*
Give to those who ask—*Matthew 5:42.*
Helping poor is lending to Lord—*Proverbs 19:17.*
The godly give generous loans—*Psalm 37:26.*

LEPROSY

Follow instructions of priests—*Deuteronomy 24:8.*
Jesus heals leper—*Matthew 8:3; Luke 5:13; 17:14.*
King Uzziah, leprosy—*2 Chronicles 26:21.*
Leper ceremonially unclean—*Leviticus 22:4.*
Lord struck king with leprosy—*2 Kings 15:5.*

LIARS/LIES

Do not lie—*Proverbs 24:28; Colossians 3:9.*
Do not pass along false reports—*Exodus 23:1.*
Do not testify falsely—*Exodus 20:16; Deuteronomy 5:20.*
From the heart comes lying—*Matthew 15:19.*
Liars die young—*Psalm 55:23.*
Liars headed for hell—*Revelation 21:8.*

Lord hates liars—*Proverbs 12:22*.

Satan tempts believers to lie—*Acts 5:3*.

LIBERTY

Be free from concerns of life—*1 Corinthians 7:32*.

Christ led captives free—*Ephesians 4:8*.

Christ purchased our freedom—*1 Timothy 2:6*.

Christ's blood freed us from sin—*Revelation 1:5*.

In Christ no slave or free—*Galatians 3:28*.

Son sets you free—*John 8:32-36*.

We are set free from law—*Romans 8:1-3*.

LIFE

Brevity of

Be mindful of brevity of life—*Psalm 39:4*.

Days are swift—*Job 7:6*.

Days on earth are like a shadow—*1 Chronicles 29:15*.

Days on earth are transient—*Job 8:9*.

Gone in a moment—*Psalm 78:39*.

Life is like morning fog—*James 4:14*.

Life passes swiftly—*Job 9:25*.

Little time left—*Job 10:20*.

Only a step away from death—*1 Samuel 20:3*.

Remember how short life is—*Psalm 89:47*.

We blossom for a moment, then wither—*Job 14:2*.

Wither like grass—*Psalm 102:11; Isaiah 40:6,7,24*.

Everlasting

All who believe in Jesus have eternal life—*John 6:47,50*.

Christ gives eternal life—*John 10:28*.

Eternal body made for us by God—*2 Corinthians 5:1*.

Eternal life, free gift of God—*Romans 6:23*.

Eternal life in Jesus—*1 John 5:11*.
Righteous will go into eternal life—*Matthew 25:46*.

LIGHT

Believers are full of light—*Ephesians 5:8*.
Children of the light—*1 Thessalonians 5:5*.
Creation, let there be light—*Genesis 1:3*.
God is light—*1 John 1:5*.
God lives in unapproachable light—*1 Timothy 6:16*.
God's Word is a lamp—*Psalm 119:105*.
Jesus' followers, light of the world—*Matthew 5:14-16*.
Jesus is the light of the world—*John 8:12; 9:5*.
Let your lives shine brightly—*Philippians 2:15*.

LITIGATION

Come to terms quickly with enemy—*Matthew 5:25*.
Do not sue Christians—*1 Corinthians 6:1*.
Try to settle the matter—*Luke 12:58*.

LOGIC

Come now, let us reason—*Isaiah 1:18; 43:26*.
Jesus confounds critics with logic—*Mark 11:29-33*.

LONELINESS

Christ is with us always—*Matthew 28:20*.
Fear not, God is with you—*Isaiah 41:10*.
God will never forsake us—*Hebrews 13:5*.
Lord is with you like a shepherd—*Psalm 23*.

LONGEVITY

Fear of Lord lengthens life—*Proverbs 10:27*.
God gives long life—*Psalm 91:16*.

Obedience to God yields long life—*Proverbs 3:2.*
Wisdom will multiply your days—*Proverbs 9:11.*

LORD'S PRAYER

Lord's Prayer—*Matthew 6:9-13; Luke 11:2-4.*

LORD'S SUPPER

Jesus celebrates—*Matthew 26:26-28; Mark 14:22-24.*
Paul on the Lord's Supper—*1 Corinthians 11:23-29.*

LOST SHEEP

Astray like a lost sheep—*Psalm 119:176; 1 Peter 2:25.*
Good shepherd seeks out—*John 10:1-27.*
Shepherd looks for single lost sheep—*Matthew 18:12.*

LOVE

For God

Be careful to love Lord—*Joshua 23:11.*
Choose to love Lord—*Deuteronomy 30:6,16,20.*
God first loved us—*1 John 4:19–5:3.*
Lord protects those who love Him—*Psalm 145:20.*
Love God, most important law—*Mark 12:29-33.*
Love God with whole heart and soul—*Deuteronomy 6:5.*
Love means doing what God commands—*2 John 6.*

Of Fellow Man

Be filled with love—*Ephesians 5:2; 1 Timothy 1:5.*
Be Good Samaritan—*Luke 10:25-37.*
Disregard people's faults—*Proverbs 17:9.*
Do everything with love—*1 Corinthians 16:14.*
Do loving deeds—*1 Thessalonians 1:3.*
Do not just pretend to love others—*Romans 12:9,10.*

Fruit of Holy Spirit, love—*Galatians 5:22.*
God commands us to love each other—*John 15:12,13.*
Golden Rule—*Matthew 7:12; Luke 6:31.*
Let love overflow—*Philippians 1:9.*
Love each other—*John 13:34,35; 15:12; Hebrews 13:1.*
Love your Christian brothers and sisters—*1 Peter 2:17.*
Love your neighbor as yourself—*James 2:8.*

LOYALTY

Be loyal to Christ—*John 14:21-24.*
Be loyal to friends—*Ruth 1:14; Proverbs 17:17; 27:6.*
Be loyal to God—*Matthew 6:24; Luke 9:62.*
Cannot serve two masters—*Matthew 6:24.*
Loyalty tested—*John 21:15-17.*

LUST

Abstain from fleshly lusts—*1 Peter 2:11.*
Avoid lust for physical pleasure—*1 John 2:16.*
Do not covet neighbor's wife—*Exodus 20:17.*
Do not even look at woman with lust—*Matthew 5:28.*
Don't gratify sinful nature—*Romans 13:14.*
Live by the Spirit to overcome lusts—*Galatians 5:16.*
Obey God, do not lust—*Proverbs 6:24,25.*
Run from youthful lusts—*2 Timothy 2:22.*

M

Magician

Magic arts—*Revelation 9:21.*
Magic charms—*Ezekiel 13:18.*
Magic spells—*Isaiah 47:12.*

Man

Creation of

All nations descended from one man—*Acts 17:26.*
Created a little lower than angels—*Psalm 8:3-6.*
Created in God's image—*Genesis 1:26,27; 9:6.*
Created in likeness of God—*Genesis 5:1; James 3:9.*
Created to live on earth—*Isaiah 45:12.*
God made male and female—*Genesis 5:2; Mark 10:6.*
God made us wonderfully complex—*Psalm 139:14.*
Man formed by God's own hands—*Job 10:8-12.*

Dichotomy View of

Man is body and soul—*Matthew 10:28.*
Man is body and spirit—*Genesis 2:7; 2 Corinthians 7:1.*
Spirit and soul equivalent—*Luke 1:46,47.*

Dominion of

Created to rule and subdue—*Genesis 1:26,28.*
Man rules over animals—*Genesis 9:2,3; Jeremiah 27:6.*
Ruler over all God's works—*Psalm 8:6.*

Insignificance of

Knows so little—*Job 38:4,12,13.*
Like a grasshopper—*Isaiah 40:22.*

Like a worm—*Job 25:6*.

What are mere mortals?—*Psalm 8:3,4; 144:3,4*.

Trichotomy View of

Man is body, soul, and spirit—*1 Thessalonians 5:23*.

Word of God divides soul and spirit—*Hebrews 4:12*.

MANNERS

Bad manners—*Judges 8:35; 1 Samuel 25:21*.

Good manners—*Leviticus 19:32; Job 29:7,8*.

MARRIAGE

Do not marry unbelievers—*2 Corinthians 6:14*.

Good wife, favor from the Lord—*Proverbs 18:22*.

Keep marriage bed pure—*Hebrews 13:4*.

Man and woman become one—*Genesis 2:24,25*.

No marriage in afterlife—*Matthew 22:30; Mark 12:25*.

Paul on marriage and divorce—*1 Corinthians 7:2-14*.

Rejoice in wife of youth—*Proverbs 5:18*.

Wife of noble character—*Proverbs 12:4; 31:10,30,31*.

Wives submit, husbands love—*Ephesians 5:22-28,33*.

MARTYRDOM

Family members may betray you—*Matthew 10:21*.

Give life up for Jesus, find true life—*Matthew 10:39*.

Martyrs under God's throne—*Revelation 6:9*.

Prophets killed—*Revelation 16:6*.

Two witnesses martyred—*Revelation 11:7*.

MARY

Mother of Jesus—*Matthew 1:16*.

Sword will pierce soul (at Jesus' crucifixion)—*Luke 2:35*.

Virgin will conceive a child—*Isaiah 7:14; Matthew 1:23*.

MATERIALISM

Cannot have two masters—*Matthew 6:24.*

Danger of greed—*1 Peter 5:2,3.*

Do not love money—*1 Timothy 3:2,3; Hebrews 13:5.*

False confidence in wealth—*Psalm 49:6; Proverbs 11:28.*

Gold a snare—*Judges 8:24-27.*

Money lovers never satisfied—*Ecclesiastes 5:10.*

Store treasure in heaven—*Matthew 6:19,20.*

MATURITY

Avoid youthful passions—*2 Timothy 2:22.*

Be steadfast—*1 Peter 5:10.*

Be strong, resist evil—*1 John 2:14.*

Content in all situations—*Philippians 4:12.*

Grow in faith and love—*2 Thessalonians 1:3.*

Grow in grace and knowledge—*2 Peter 3:18.*

Grow to completion—*Philippians 1:6.*

Mature through Scripture—*2 Timothy 3:16,17.*

Put away childish things—*1 Corinthians 13:11.*

Stand firm—*Philippians 1:27-30.*

Think like adults—*1 Corinthians 14:20.*

MEDICINE

Cheerful heart is good medicine—*Proverbs 17:22.*

Healing leaves in heaven—*Revelation 22:2.*

Medicinal wine—*1 Timothy 5:23.*

Ointments, bandages—*Isaiah 1:6; 38:21.*

Strong drink for the dying—*Proverbs 31:6.*

MEDITATION

Meditate on God's Law—*Joshua 1:8.*

Meditate on God's principles—*Psalm 119:23,48*.
Meditate through the night—*Psalm 63:6*.
Ponder God's great works—*Psalm 143:5*.
Reflect on God's ways—*Psalm 119:15*.

MEEKNESS

Avoid conceit—*Galatians 5:26*.
Be humble and gentle—*Ephesians 4:2*.
Clothe yourselves with humility—*Colossians 3:12*.
God blesses the gentle and lowly—*Matthew 5:5*.
God leads the humble—*Psalm 25:9*.
Humble will be filled with fresh joy—*Isaiah 29:19*.

MERCY

Clothe yourselves with mercy—*Colossians 3:12*.
God blesses the merciful—*Matthew 5:7*.
God's mercy and compassion—*Deuteronomy 4:31*.
God's mercy to those who fear Him—*Luke 1:50*.
New mercies every morning—*Lamentations 3:22,24*.
Those who confess sins find mercy—*Proverbs 28:13*.

MESSIAH

God's Chosen One, the Messiah—*Luke 23:35*.
Inaugurates New Covenant—*Jeremiah 31:31-34*.
Jesus is Messiah—*Matthew 1:1; 16:20; Luke 9:20; 23:2*.
Miracles prove Jesus is Messiah—*John 20:31*.
Prophecy of Messiah as God—*Isaiah 40:3; Matthew 3:3*.
Redeems from sin—*1 Peter 1:18-20*.
To be born in Bethlehem—*Micah 5:2*.
To be born of a virgin—*Isaiah 7:14; Matthew 1:23*.
Work of Messiah described—*Isaiah 53*.

MILITARY

Devout centurion—*Acts 10:1,2,22.*
God, a military leader—*Judges 3:1,2.*
Soldiers of Christ—*2 Timothy 2:1-4.*
Soldiers pierced Jesus' side—*John 19:34.*
War in heaven—*Revelation 12:7.*

MILLENNIAL KINGDOM

1000-year period, Christ rules—*Revelation 20:1-3.*
Time of full knowledge of Lord—*Isaiah 11:9.*
Time of peace—*Isaiah 19:24,25.*
Time of righteousness—*Isaiah 11:4.*

MINISTRY

Build up church—*2 Corinthians 12:19.*
Entrusted with gospel—*1 Thessalonians 2:4.*
Exhort Christians—*Titus 1:9; 2:15.*
Feed believers—*Acts 20:28; 1 Peter 5:2.*
Issue warnings—*Acts 20:30,31.*
Preach the gospel—*1 Corinthians 1:17.*
Strengthen faith—*Acts 14:22.*
Teach doctrine—*2 Timothy 2:2.*
Watch over souls—*Hebrews 13:17.*

MIRACLES

Convincing Effect of

Crowds listened intently—*Acts 8:6.*
Disciples believed in Christ—*John 2:11,22,23.*
God convinces by miracles—*Romans 15:19.*
Prove that Jesus is Messiah—*John 20:31.*

Of the New Testament, Notable
5000 fed—*Matthew 14:15-21*.
Fig tree withered—*Matthew 21:18-22*.
Lazarus raised from the dead—*John 11:38-44*.
Net full of fishes—*Luke 5:1-11*.
Ten lepers cleansed—*Luke 17:11-19*.
Walking on water—*Matthew 14:25-33*.
Water turned into wine—*John 2:1-11*.
Windstorm stilled—*Matthew 8:23-27*.

Of the Old Testament, Notable
Daniel in lion's den—*Daniel 6:22*.
God divides sea—*Exodus 14:13-22*.
Jonah swallowed by great fish—*Jonah 1:17*.
Lord appeared in burning bush—*Exodus 3:2*.
Lot's wife became pillar of salt—*Genesis 19:26*.
Moses' staff became snake—*Exodus 4:3-5*.
Shadrach and friends in furnace—*Daniel 3:19-30*.
Sun stands still—*Joshua 10:12,13*.

MISSIONARY WORK
Be ready with an answer—*1 Peter 3:15*.
Christ's ambassadors—*2 Corinthians 5:18-21*.
Contend for faith—*Jude 3*.
Evangelize—*Matthew 28:19,20*.
Message of missionaries—*1 Timothy 2:5-7*.
Message to entire world—*Acts 10:9-20*.
Paul's first journey—*Acts 13–14*.
Paul's second journey—*Acts 15–18:22*.
Paul's third journey—*Acts 18:23–21:15*.
Spread of gospel—*Colossians 1:6*.

MIXED MARRIAGES (BELIEVERS WITH UNBELIEVERS)

Bad results—*Genesis 6:1-4.*

Don't be yoked with unbeliever—*2 Corinthians 6:14-16.*

Two cannot walk together unless agreed—*Amos 3:3.*

MOCKING

Am I my brother's keeper?—*Genesis 4:9.*

Go away, you baldhead—*2 Kings 2:23.*

Hail! King of the Jews—*John 19:3.*

Rebuild temple in three days, can you?—*Mark 15:29.*

You would convert me?—*Acts 26:28.*

MODEL

Be example by doing good deeds—*Titus 2:7.*

Do not be influenced by bad example—*3 John 11.*

Do not be stumbling block—*1 Corinthians 8:9,13.*

Imitate apostles and Lord—*1 Thessalonians 1:6.*

Imitate church leaders—*Hebrews 13:7.*

Imitate the ants—*Proverbs 6:6,9.*

MODESTY

Examples of—*1 Samuel 9:21; Esther 1:11,12; Job 32:4-7.*

Women should be modest—*1 Timothy 2:9.*

MONEY

Cannot buy gift of God—*Acts 8:20.*

Cannot have two masters—*Matthew 6:24.*

Dishonest money dwindles—*Proverbs 13:11.*

Do not be greedy for money—*1 Peter 5:2.*

Do not love money—*1 Timothy 3:2,3; Hebrews 13:5.*

Money lovers never satisfied—*Ecclesiastes 5:10.*

MONOTHEISM

God is one—*James 2:19.*

Lord is one—*Deuteronomy 6:4.*

One God and Father of all—*Ephesians 4:5,6.*

There is no God but one—*1 Corinthians 8:4.*

MORALITY

Bad company corrupts character—*1 Corinthians 15:33.*

Be holy for God is holy—*1 Peter 1:15.*

Fruit of Holy Spirit—*Galatians 5:22,23.*

Kingdom of God requires—*Romans 14:17.*

Morality in Sermon on the Mount—*Matthew 5–7.*

Morality in Ten Commandments—*Exodus 20:1-17.*

MORTALITY

All people die—*Job 30:23; Ecclesiastes 7:2.*

Death resulted from sin—*Romans 5:12.*

Each person dies once—*Hebrews 9:27.*

Man is like withering grass—*Psalm 90:5,6; 103:15,16.*

No one has power over death—*Ecclesiastes 8:8.*

Return to ground—*Genesis 3:19.*

We quickly disappear—*Job 14:1,2.*

MOSES

Commissioned to deliver Israelites—*Exodus 3:10.*

God appeared to in burning bush—*Exodus 3:2.*

"Let my people go"—*Exodus 5:1.*

Stone tablets, Ten Commandments—*Exodus 34:29.*

Was taught all the wisdom of the Egyptians—*Acts 7:22.*

MOTHER

Do not neglect mother's teaching—*Proverbs 1:8; 6:20.*

Honor your mother—*Exodus 20:12; Matthew 19:19.*
Love Jesus more than mother—*Matthew 10:37.*
Respect mother—*Leviticus 19:3.*

MURDER

Capital punishment instituted for murder—*Genesis 9:6.*
Commandment against murder—*Exodus 20:13.*
From the heart comes murder—*Matthew 15:19.*
God abhors murderers and deceivers—*Psalm 5:6.*
God will avenge—*Deuteronomy 32:43; Psalm 9:12.*
Lord detests murderers—*Psalm 5:6.*
Murder comes from sin nature—*Galatians 5:21.*
Murderers do not have eternal life—*1 John 3:15.*

MURMURING

Against Christ—*Luke 5:30; John 6:41-43,52.*
Against God—*Proverbs 19:3.*
Angers God—*Numbers 14:2,11; Deuteronomy 9:8,22.*
Do not grumble—*1 Corinthians 10:10.*
Stay away from complaining—*Philippians 2:14.*

MUSIC AND MUSICAL INSTRUMENTS

Hymns and spiritual songs—*Colossians 3:16.*
Praise God with—*Psalm 43:4; 71:22; 98:5; 144:9.*
Prayer accompanied by—*Habakkuk 3:19.*
Promotes joy—*Ecclesiastes 2:8-10.*
Song of Moses—*Exodus 15:1-18.*
Used at coronation of kings—*2 Chronicles 23:11-13.*
Used at religious feasts—*2 Chronicles 30:21.*
Used in Temple—*1 Chronicles 16:4-6.*
Used to celebrate victory—*1 Samuel 18:6,7.*

NAMES OF GOD

El Elyon is the Most High—*Isaiah 14:13,14.*
El Olam is the Everlasting God—*Isaiah 40:28.*
El Roi is the Strong One who sees us—*Genesis 16:13.*
El Shaddai is God Almighty—*Genesis 17:1-21.*
Elohim created the universe—*Genesis 1:1.*
Elohim is Yahweh—*Deuteronomy 6:4.*
Yahweh delivered Israel from Egypt—*Exodus 20:2.*
Yahweh-Jireh provides for us—*Genesis 22:13,14.*
Yahweh-Sabbaoth is the Lord of hosts—*1 Samuel 1:3.*
Yahweh-Shalom is our peace—*Judges 6:24.*
Yahweh-Shammah is present with us—*Ezekiel 48:35.*

NATIONS

Every nation came from one man—*Acts 17:26.*
God has plan for whole earth—*Isaiah 14:26.*
God has plans for Israel—*Romans 9–11.*
Nations will beat swords into plowshares—*Isaiah 2:4.*
What joy for nation whose God is the Lord—*Psalm 33:12.*

NATURE, WORLD OF

All nature praises God—*1 Chronicles 16:31-33.*
Beautiful flowers—*Song of Solomon 2:12.*
Christ upholds creation—*Colossians 1:17.*
Earth entrusted to man—*Psalm 115:16.*
New heavens, new earth—*Isaiah 65:17; 66:22.*
Not even Solomon dressed like lilies—*Matthew 6:29.*
Revelation through nature—*Psalm 19:1-14.*
Wilderness will rejoice and blossom—*Isaiah 35:1.*

NAZARETH

Can anything good come from Nazareth?—*John 1:46.*
God sent angel Gabriel to Nazareth—*Luke 1:26,27.*
Jesus, a Nazarene—*Matthew 2:23; Mark 1:24.*

NECROMANCY

Consulting mediums and psychics—*Isaiah 8:19.*
Do not call forth the dead—*Deuteronomy 18:10-12.*
Medium at Endor—*1 Samuel 28:7.*

NEIGHBOR

Do not plot against neighbors—*Proverbs 3:29.*
Do not testify falsely against neighbor—*Exodus 20:16.*
Love your neighbor as yourself—*Matthew 19:19; 22:39.*

NEW HEAVENS AND NEW EARTH

New heavens, new earth—*Isaiah 65:17; 66:22.*

NIGHT

Darkness was called night—*Genesis 1:5.*
Jesus prayed to God all night—*Luke 6:12.*
Meditating on God during night—*Psalm 63:6.*
No night in heaven—*Revelation 22:5.*
Ponder God's promises during night—*Psalm 119:148.*

NOAH

Entered the Ark—*Genesis 7:1.*
Lived 350 years after flood—*Genesis 9:28.*
Lived to 950 years old—*Genesis 9:29.*
Made the Ark—*Genesis 6:14.*

OBEDIENCE

Be careful to obey everything—*Joshua 23:6.*
Be devoted to obedience—*Psalm 119:45.*
Blessed are those that obey—*Psalm 119:2,12.*
God loves the obedient—*Deuteronomy 5:10.*
Happiness and obedience—*Psalm 112:1; 119:55,56.*
Hurry to obey—*Psalm 119:60.*
Jesus' obedience—*John 4:34.*
Obedience and long life—*1 Kings 3:14.*
Obedience better than sacrifice—*1 Samuel 15:22.*
Obey and all will be well—*Jeremiah 7:23.*
Obey and live forever—*John 8:51; 1 John 2:17.*
Obey God over humans—*Acts 4:19; 5:29.*
Obey wholeheartedly—*Joshua 24:14; Romans 6:17.*

OBESITY

Gluttony—*Proverbs 23:2.*
Gorging—*Proverbs 23:20,21.*
Overeating—*Proverbs 25:16.*
Stomach is god—*Philippians 3:19.*

OBSCENITY

Avoid foul or abusive language—*Romans 3:13,14.*
Avoid perverse talk—*Proverbs 4:24.*
Do not speak evil—*James 4:11; 1 Peter 3:10.*
Mouths full of cursing, lies, and threats—*Psalm 10:7.*
Obscene stories and coarse jokes—*Ephesians 5:4.*
Wicked speak only what is corrupt—*Proverbs 10:32.*

OCCULTISM

Astrologers cannot save you—*Isaiah 47:13.*
Consulting mediums brings judgment—*Leviticus 20:6.*
Diviners will be disgraced—*Micah 3:7.*
Do not call forth the dead—*Deuteronomy 18:11.*
Do not listen to fortunetellers—*Jeremiah 27:9.*
Do not listen to mediums, psychics—*Leviticus 19:31.*
Do not practice fortunetelling—*Leviticus 19:26.*
Do not try to read future in stars—*Jeremiah 10:2.*
Execute mediums, psychics, sorcerers—*Exodus 22:18.*
Medium at Endor—*1 Samuel 28:7.*
No fortunetelling or sorcery—*Deuteronomy 18:10,11.*
Saul consulted medium—*1 Chronicles 10:13.*

OFFERINGS

Figurative

Give your bodies to God—*Romans 12:1.*
Sacrifice of praise—*Hebrews 13:15.*

Piety Must Accompany

Broken spirit desired—*Psalm 51:17.*
Do what is right—*Proverbs 21:3.*
No hypocrisy—*Amos 5:21.*
Obedience required—*1 Samuel 15:22.*

OLD AGE

Extended age prior to flood—*Genesis 6:3.*
God sustains us even in old age—*Isaiah 46:4.*
Gray hair is a crown of glory—*Proverbs 16:31.*
Satisfying long life—*Psalm 91:16.*
Seventy years are given to us—*Psalm 90:10.*
Wisdom belongs to the aged—*Job 12:12.*

OPPOSITION

By family members—*Matthew 10:21*.
By powers of darkness—*Ephesians 6:12*.
By the devil—*1 Thessalonians 2:18; 1 Peter 5:8,9*.
Gently teach those who oppose truth—*2 Timothy 2:25*.
Godly suffer persecution—*2 Timothy 3:12*.
Opposition to Christ—*Matthew 26:3,4*.
Opposition to God—*2 Thessalonians 2:3,4*.
Opposition to Holy Spirit—*Acts 7:51*.
Opposition to ministry—*1 Corinthians 16:9*.
Opposition to those who speak truth—*Isaiah 30:10*.
Pray for those who persecute you—*Romans 12:14*.
Soft speech crushes opposition—*Proverbs 25:15*.
When God is for us…—*Romans 8:31*.

OPPRESSION

Do not oppress foreigners—*Exodus 22:21; 23:9*.
Do not oppress widows, orphans—*Zechariah 7:10*.
God rescues the oppressed—*Psalm 9:9; 12:5*.
Lord helps those treated unfairly—*Psalm 103:6*.
Oppression and extortion wrong—*Habakkuk 2:6*.

OPTIMISM

Be confident—*2 Corinthians 5:6*.
Be joyful always—*1 Thessalonians 5:16*.
Be strong and take heart—*Psalm 31:24*.
God has plans for us—*Jeremiah 29:10,11*.
Hope in God—*Psalm 42:5*.
Let us rejoice and be glad—*Psalm 118:24*.
No fear of bad news—*Psalm 112:7,8*.
There is a future—*Psalm 37:37*.

PAGAN PRACTICES

Detestable acts—*Deuteronomy 12:31.*

Human sacrifice in fire—*2 Kings 16:3; 17:17.*

Idolatry—*Deuteronomy 27:15.*

Indulgence in pagan revelry—*1 Corinthians 10:7.*

Sacrifice of sons and daughters—*Psalm 106:37.*

Sacrifices to demons—*Deuteronomy 32:17.*

Sacrificing to false god—*Exodus 22:20.*

Sorcery and divination—*2 Kings 21:6.*

PARADISE

Paul caught up to paradise—*2 Corinthians 12:4.*

Thief with Christ in paradise—*Luke 23:43.*

Tree of life in paradise—*Revelation 2:7.*

PARENTS

Bring children to Christ—*Matthew 19:13,14.*

Do not provoke children—*Ephesians 6:4.*

Even if parents forsake you, God will not—*Psalm 27:10.*

Good influence over children—*1 Kings 9:4.*

Listen to what parents teach—*Proverbs 1:8; 6:20; 23:22.*

Parents correct children—*Proverbs 13:24; 19:18; 22:15.*

Parents exercise control over children—*1 Timothy 3:4.*

Parents nurture children—*Ephesians 6:4.*

Parents provide for children—*2 Corinthians 12:14.*

Parents the pride of their children—*Proverbs 17:6.*

Partiality of parents—*Genesis 25:28; 37:3; 48:22.*

Pray for children—*1 Thessalonians 5:17.*

Show compassion to children—*Psalm 103:13*.
Treat children fairly—*Deuteronomy 21:15-17*.

PASSOVER

Celebrate Passover—*Ezekiel 45:21*.
Christ, our Passover Lamb—*1 Corinthians 5:7*.
Jesus' betrayal, near time of Passover—*Matthew 26:2*.

PASTOR

Appointed by God—*2 Corinthians 3:6; 4:1; 5:18*.
Feed and shepherd God's flock—*Acts 20:28; 1 Peter 5:2*.
Not heavy drinker—*1 Timothy 3:3; Titus 1:7*.
Not lover of money—*1 Timothy 3:3*.
Not quick-tempered—*Titus 1:7*.
Pray over the sick—*James 5:14*.
Pray, preach, and teach—*Acts 6:4*.
Preach the Word—*Mark 16:15; 1 Timothy 4:2,13*.
Set example for flock—*1 Peter 5:3*.

PATIENCE

Be patient in trouble—*Romans 12:12*.
Be patient until Lord's coming—*James 5:7-10*.
Be patient with everyone—*Ephesians 4:2*.
Clothe yourselves in patience—*Colossians 3:12*.
Do not be quick-tempered—*Ecclesiastes 7:8,9*.
Fruit of Spirit includes patience—*Galatians 5:22*.
Love is patient—*1 Corinthians 13:4*.
Patient endurance—*2 Corinthians 1:6; 2 Peter 1:6*.
Patiently endure unfair treatment—*1 Peter 2:19*.
Wait patiently for Lord—*Psalm 37:7*.

PAUL

Apostle—*1 Corinthians 9:1*.

Educated under Gamaliel—*Acts 22:3.*
Jew of Tarsus—*Acts 21:39.*
Lord appears to Paul—*Acts 9:3-9.*
Member of Pharisees—*Philippians 3:5.*

PEACE OF MIND

Be at peace, Christ has overcome world—*John 16:33.*
Fruit of Holy Spirit—*Galatians 5:22.*
Let not your heart be troubled—*John 14:27.*
Let peace of God rule your heart—*Colossians 3:15.*
Mind stayed on God is in perfect peace—*Isaiah 26:3.*
Peace and joy in the Holy Spirit—*Romans 14:17.*
Peace of God guards your heart—*Philippians 4:7.*

PENITENCE

God answers prayers of the penitent—*2 Chronicles 7:14.*
God comforts the penitent—*Matthew 5:4.*
God forgives the penitent—*Micah 7:18.*
Lord is close to the brokenhearted—*Psalm 34:18.*

PENTECOST

Holy Spirit fell on Day of Pentecost—*Acts 2.*

PERFECTION

✗ Be perfect—*Matthew 5:48.*
Believers do not claim perfection—*Philippians 3:12.*
Church will attain to perfection—*Ephesians 4:13.*
God's law is perfect—*Psalm 19:7.*
God's power made perfect in weakness—*2 Corinthians 12:9.*
Impossibility of attaining perfection—*Psalm 119:96.*
Perfect faithfulness of God—*Isaiah 25:1.*

Perfect in Christ—*1 Corinthians 2:6; Philippians 3:15*.
Pray for perfection—*Hebrews 13:20,21; 1 Peter 5:10*.

PERJURY

Do not lie—*Leviticus 19:11*.
Do not pass along false reports—*Exodus 23:1*.
Do not testify falsely—*Exodus 20:16; Deuteronomy 5:20*.
False witness tells lies—*Proverbs 12:17*.
Perjurers—*1 Timothy 1:10*.

PERSECUTION

All the godly suffer persecution—*2 Timothy 3:12*.
Blessed are those persecuted for righteousness—
    Matthew 5:10,11.
Do not be surprised if world hates you—*1 John 3:13*.
God blesses those mocked for following Jesus—*Luke 6:22,23*.
Rejoice in being counted worthy to suffer—*Acts 5:41*.
Suffer with Christ now, be glorified with Christ
    later—*Romans 8:17*.
You will be persecuted—*Revelation 2:10*.

PERSEVERANCE

Be faithful to the end—*Hebrews 3:14*.
Do not tire of doing good—*Galatians 6:9*.
Endure suffering—*2 Timothy 2:3*.
Hold on to what is good—*1 Thessalonians 5:21*.
Hold tightly to hope—*Hebrews 10:23*.
Remain faithful—*2 Timothy 3:14*.
Run with endurance—*Hebrews 12:1*.
Stand firm—*2 Corinthians 1:21; Ephesians 6:13*.

Stand true—*1 Corinthians 16:13.*

Watch out for attacks from devil—*1 Peter 5:8.*

Watch out, avoid error—*2 Peter 3:17.*

PESSIMISM

All is meaningless—*Ecclesiastes 1:2.*

Dread fulfilled—*Job 3:25.*

Focusing on affliction—*Psalm 116:10,11.*

Focusing on troubles—*Psalm 25:17.*

PHARISEES

Brood of snakes—*Matthew 3:7.*

Hypocrites—*Matthew 6:2; Luke 12:1.*

Tried to trap Jesus—*Matthew 19:3; 22:15.*

Worship is a farce—*Matthew 15:9.*

PHILOSOPHY

Empty philosophy—*Colossians 2:8.*

Epicurean and Stoic philosophers—*Acts 17:18.*

High-sounding ideas—*1 Corinthians 1:17.*

Human wisdom—*1 Corinthians 1:19,21,22; 2:13.*

Wisdom that belongs to this world—*1 Corinthians 2:6.*

PHYSICIAN

Doctor Luke—*Colossians 4:14.*

Physician, heal yourself—*Luke 4:23.*

Sick people need a doctor—*Matthew 9:12; Mark 2:17.*

PLEASURE, WORLDLY

Constant partying injurious—*Isaiah 5:11-13.*

Fools think only about fun—*Ecclesiastes 7:4.*

Love of pleasure leads to poverty—*Proverbs 21:17.*

Pleasures of life can stifle spiritual interests—*Luke 8:14*.

Sin nature craves for pleasures—*Galatians 5:19-21*.

Slaves to evil pleasures—*Titus 3:3*.

Worldly pleasures do not satisfy—*Ecclesiastes 2:8-11*.

POLITICS

Corruption—*Psalm 12:8; Daniel 6:4-15*.

Electioneering—*2 Samuel 15:2-6*.

End-time government—*Revelation 17:12.*

God controls governments—*Romans 13:1*.

Obey government—*Romans 13:1,5*.

Politicians should be diligent—*Romans 12:8*.

Pray for kings and others in authority—*1 Timothy 2:2*.

Submit to government—*Titus 3:1*.

Wicked ruler is dangerous—*Proverbs 28:15*.

POLYGAMY

Church leaders, faithful to one wife—*1 Timothy 3:2,12*.

Solomon loved many foreign women—*1 Kings 11:1-4*.

POLYTHEISM

False gods—*Isaiah 2:8; Jeremiah 2:11*.

Many so-called gods—*1 Corinthians 8:5*.

POOR

Duty to

Be kind to the poor—*Psalm 41:1*.

Feed the hungry—*Isaiah 58:7,10*.

Give generously to others in need—*Ephesians 4:28*.

Give helping hand to the poor—*Proverbs 31:20*.

Help the oppressed—*Isaiah 1:17*.

Share money generously—*Romans 12:8*.

Oppression of

Borrower is servant to lender—*Proverbs 22:7.*

Deprivation of the poor—*Isaiah 10:2.*

Poor are despised—*Proverbs 14:20.*

Poor are kicked aside—*Job 24:4.*

Robbery of the poor—*Amos 8:4.*

Trampling the poor—*Amos 5:11.*

POPULARITY

Better to be sincere—*Colossians 3:22.*

Love for praise of men—*John 12:43.*

POVERTY

Better to be poor and godly—*Proverbs 16:8.*

Give me neither poverty nor riches—*Proverbs 30:8.*

Love sleep, end in poverty—*Proverbs 20:13.*

Playing around brings poverty—*Proverbs 28:19.*

POWER

All-surpassing power is from God—*2 Corinthians 4:7.*

Be strong in Lord's power—*Ephesians 6:10.*

God gives power to weak—*Isaiah 40:29; 2 Peter 1:3.*

God gives us spirit of power—*2 Timothy 1:7,8.*

God's power made perfect in weakness—*2 Corinthians 12:9.*

Power from Holy Spirit—*Acts 1:8; Ephesians 3:16.*

Power of the Most High—*Luke 1:35.*

Of Christ

Authority over everything—*John 3:35.*

Disarmed evil rulers and authorities—*Colossians 2:15.*

Holds all creation together—*Colossians 1:17.*

Overcame the world—*John 16:33*.
Resurrection—*John 2:19; 10:18*.
Sustains universe—*Hebrews 1:3*.
Wind and waves obey Him—*Matthew 8:27*.

Of God

All-powerful—*Job 36:22*.
Be strong with the Lord's power—*Ephesians 6:10*.
Made the earth by His power—*Jeremiah 10:12*.
Miracles—*1 Chronicles 16:9*.
Nothing is too hard—*Genesis 18:14;*
Jeremiah 32:27.
Performs miracles without number—*Job 5:9*.
Spread out the heavens above—*Isaiah 48:13*.
With God everything is possible—*Matthew 19:26*.

Of the Holy Spirit

Begot Jesus—*Luke 1:35*.
Jesus filled by Spirit's power—*Luke 4:14*.
Power from the Holy Spirit—*Acts 1:8; Acts 2*.
Raised Jesus from the dead—*Romans 8:11*.
Spirit fills believers with power—*Luke 24:49; Acts 1:8*.

PRAISE

Give thanks always—*Ephesians 5:20*.
Give thanks to the Lord—*1 Chronicles 16:8*.
Let all things praise the Lord—*Psalm 103:1-5,20-22*.
Offer sacrifice of praise—*Hebrews 13:15*.
Sing a new song to the Lord—*Psalm 96:1; 98:1*.
Sing songs of praise—*James 5:13*.
Worship Lord with gladness—*Psalm 100*.

PRAYER

Ask and it will be given—*Matthew 7:7,8.*

Ask in Jesus' name—*John 14:13,14.*

Believe and you will receive—*Matthew 21:22.*

Earnest prayer—*James 5:17,18.*

Lift up hands in prayer—*1 Timothy 2:8.*

Pray and seek God's face—*2 Chronicles 7:14.*

PRAYERFULNESS

Always be prayerful—*Romans 12:12.*

Daniel prayed three times a day—*Daniel 6:10.*

Keep on praying—*1 Thessalonians 5:17.*

Pray as long as you have breath—*Psalm 116:2.*

PREACHING

Be persistent in preaching—*2 Timothy 4:2.*

Builds believers up—*Ephesians 4:11,12.*

Called to preach—*2 Timothy 1:11.*

Compulsion to preach—*1 Corinthians 9:16.*

Faithfully preach truth—*2 Corinthians 6:7-9.*

Preach about righteousness—*Acts 24:25.*

Preach Christ crucified—*1 Corinthians 1:23.*

Preach with sincerity—*2 Corinthians 2:17.*

Preach Jesus as Lord—*2 Corinthians 4:5.*

Preach the Word—*Mark 16:15,16; Ephesians 6:20.*

Preach without fear—*Ephesians 6:19,20.*

PREDESTINATION

Father gave followers to Jesus—*John 6:39.*

God chose us in Christ—*Ephesians 1:4.*

God has a prearranged plan—*Acts 2:23.*

God's plan is from all eternity—*Ephesians 3:11*.
Many are called, few are chosen—*Matthew 22:14*.
Planned long before the world began—*2 Timothy 1:9*.

PRIDE

Better to be lowly in spirit—*Proverbs 16:19*.
Do not be conceited—*Romans 12:16*.
God humbles the proud—*Isaiah 13:11; Daniel 4:37*.
God opposes the proud—*James 4:6; 1 Peter 5:5*.
Pride goes before destruction—*Proverbs 16:18; 18:12*.
Pride is sinful—*Proverbs 21:4*.

PRIEST

Beautiful garments—*Exodus 28:2*.
Cleansing of—*Leviticus 16:24*.
Must be purified—*Exodus 19:22*.
Never be defiled—*Ezekiel 44:25,26*.

PRIORITY

Better to be a servant than ambitious—*Luke 22:26*.
Better to be free from concerns—*1 Corinthians 7:32,33*.
Better to be godly and have little—*Psalm 37:16*.
Better to lose one part of body—*Matthew 5:29,30*.
God and His will, top priority—*Matthew 6:33*.
Good reputation better than riches—*Proverbs 22:1*.
Kingdom more important—*Luke 18:29,30*.
Living is for Christ, dying better—*Philippians 1:21*.
More blessed to give—*Acts 20:35*.
Obedience better than sacrifice—*1 Samuel 15:22*.
Store up treasure in heaven—*Luke 12:33*.

PROOFS OF GOD'S EXISTENCE

Creation proves a Creator—*Psalm 19:1-4; Hebrews 3:4.*

Design of universe proves Designer—*Romans 1:18-20.*

Human personhood proves Divine Person—*Acts 17:29.*

PROPITIATION

Jesus took our punishment—*Romans 3:25.*

Peace with God through Christ—*Romans 5:1.*

Reconciled—*2 Corinthians 5:10,11,18,19.*

Took away our sins—*1 John 2:2.*

PROSPERITY

Danger of—*Psalm 73:12; Mark 10:24; Luke 18:25.*

God blesses, prospers you—*Deuteronomy 28:8.*

God prospers the humble—*Job 5:11.*

Hard work means prosperity—*Proverbs 12:11.*

Trusting Lord leads to prosperity—*Proverbs 28:25.*

Wicked prosper—*Job 21:7.*

PROVIDENCE

Of God in Circumstances

All things work for good—*Romans 8:28.*

Father cares for us—*Matthew 10:29-31.*

Joseph betrayed by brothers, led to good—*Genesis 45:8.*

Length of life—*Job 14:5; Psalm 139:16.*

Of God in History

Controls nations—*Job 12:23,24; Psalm 22:28.*

Determines when people are born—*Acts 17:25-27.*

Divine plan—*Acts 4:27,28.*

Sets up kings, deposes them—*Daniel 2:21.*

Of God in Nature

Birds are fed—*Matthew 6:26, Psalm 147:9.*
Grass grows for cattle—*Psalm 104:14.*
Sends rain—*Job 5:10; Psalm 65:9,10; 147:8.*

PROVISIONS

God is sufficient—*2 Corinthians 9:8.*
God always provides—*Isaiah 58:11.*
God will supply all needs—*Philippians 4:19.*
Seek first God's kingdom—*Matthew 6:33.*

PRUDENCE

Prudent consider their steps—*Proverbs 14:8,15,16.*
Prudent man keeps quiet—*Amos 5:13.*
Prudent person foresees danger—*Proverbs 22:3; 27:12.*

PUBLIC OPINION

Priests feared Jesus' popularity—*Mark 11:18.*
Seek God's approval—*John 12:42,43.*

PUNISHMENT

According to Deeds

God gives people their due rewards—*Jeremiah 17:10.*
God gives what is deserved—*Ezekiel 16:59.*
God repays people according to deeds—*Job 34:11.*

Delayed

God delays His wrath—*Isaiah 48:9.*
God delays punishment—*1 Kings 21:29.*
God waited patiently—*1 Peter 3:20.*

Eternal

Eternal fire—*Matthew 25:41.*

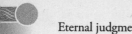

Eternal judgment—*Hebrews 6:2.*
Eternal punishment—*Matthew 25:46.*

PURITY OF HEART

God blesses those with pure hearts—*Matthew 5:8.*
Keep yourself pure—*1 Timothy 5:22.*
Purify your hearts—*2 Corinthians 7:1; James 4:8.*

QUARREL

Act quickly to settle—*Matthew 5:25*.

Anger causes quarrels—*Proverbs 30:33*.

Constant quarrels—*Proverbs 18:6*.

Contentiousness—*Psalm 120:7; 140:2; Proverbs 15:18*.

Family quarrels—*Genesis 21:10; Proverbs 18:19; 19:13*.

RACE

Ethnic

All nations descended from one man—*Acts 17:26*.

Eve, mother of all people—*Genesis 3:20*.

We are all children of the same Father—*Malachi 2:10*.

Spiritual

Do not lose the race—*Philippians 2:16*.

Keep your eyes on Jesus (the finish line)—*Hebrews 12:2*.

Run in way that you will win—*1 Corinthians 9:24*.

RAIN

Disobey, and God withholds rain—*Deuteronomy 11:17*.

Elijah prevented rain—*James 5:17*.

God directs rain to fall—*Job 37:6*.

Obedience brings God's seasonal rains—*Isaiah 30:23*.

RAPTURE OF CHURCH

All will be changed—*1 Corinthians 15:50-52*.

Christ will bring raptured church to place He prepared—*John 14:1-3*.

Church delivered from trouble—*Revelation 3:10*.

Church not appointed to wrath—*1 Thessalonians 1:10*.

Church will be raptured—*1 Thessalonians 4:13-17*.

RASHNESS

Do not be quick-tempered—*Ecclesiastes 7:9*.

Do not make rash promises to God—*Ecclesiastes 5:2*.

Do not speak without thinking—*Proverbs 29:20*.

Hasty temper yields mistakes—*Proverbs 14:29*.

Reasoning

Be ready with answer—*1 Peter 3:15.*
Come now, let us reason—*Isaiah 1:18; 43:26.*

Rebellion

Joy for those whose rebellion is forgiven—*Psalm 32:1,2.*
Lord, show me my rebellion—*Job 13:23.*
Rebellion against God—*1 Samuel 15:23; Psalm 68:6.*
Rebellion is as bad as sin of witchcraft—*1 Samuel 15:23.*
Rebels from earliest childhood—*Isaiah 48:8.*

Rebuke

Open rebuke better than hidden love—*Proverbs 27:5.*
Patiently correct, rebuke—*2 Timothy 4:2.*
Rebuke when necessary—*Titus 1:13.*
Rebuking a fool—*Proverbs 26:5.*
Warn each other—*Hebrews 3:13.*

Reconciliation Between God and Man

Made right in God's sight—*Romans 5:1.*
Reconciled through Christ—*2 Corinthians 5:18.*
Restored to friendship with God—*Romans 5:10.*

Recreation

Get away and rest—*Mark 6:31,32.*
Physical rest commanded—*Exodus 23:12; Leviticus 23:3.*

Redemption

Redeemed from bondage of law—*Galatians 4:5.*
Redeemed from death—*Hosea 13:14.*
Redeemed from evil world—*Galatians 1:13-15.*
Redeemed from grave—*Psalm 49:15.*

Redeemed from sin—*Titus 2:14*.
Redemption through Christ—*Romans 3:24*.

REFUGE

God is our hiding place—*Psalm 32:7*.
God is our refuge—*Deuteronomy 33:27; Psalm 27:5*.
God is our rock and fortress—*Psalm 71:3*.
Godly have a refuge when they die—*Proverbs 14:32*.
Happy are those who take refuge in God—*Psalm 34:8*.

REGENERATION

God creates clean heart—*Psalm 51:10*.
God creates new hearts—*Ezekiel 36:26,27*.
God creates tender hearts—*Ezekiel 11:19*.
God removes all impurities—*Isaiah 1:25*.
God writes law on hearts—*Jeremiah 31:33*.
Jesus gives living water—*John 4:10*.
Jesus is a life-giving vine—*John 15:1,3*.
New birth—*John 3:1-5; 1 Peter 1:23*.

RELATIONSHIPS

Caution in friendship—*Proverbs 12:26*.
Do not forsake friend—*Proverbs 27:10*.
Friend loves at all times—*Proverbs 17:17*.
Husband and wife, marriage—*Genesis 2:23,24*.
Husbands, love your wives—*Colossians 3:19*.
Husbands, one wife only—*1 Timothy 3:2-5*.
Lay down life for friends—*John 15:13-15*.
Love your neighbor—*Matthew 22:39; John 13:35*.
Relationships with believers—*Matthew 25:40*.
Wife is her husband's joy—*Proverbs 12:4*.

RELIGION

False

Clean outside, dirty inside—*Matthew 23:25-28*.

Hypocrites tithe, but no religion—*Matthew 23:23*.

Just going through the motions—*Hosea 6:6*.

Leaving Christ out of the picture—*John 5:39,40*.

Legalism—*Matthew 12:1-8*.

"Lord, Lord"—*Matthew 7:21-23*.

Mere lip service—*Mark 7:6,7*.

True

Fear God, keep His commandments—*Ecclesiastes 12:13*.

Fear God, walk in His ways—*Deuteronomy 10:12,13*.

Look after orphans and widows—*James 1:27*.

Love everyone—*Romans 13:10*.

Love God with whole heart—*Mark 12:33*.

Walk humbly—*Micah 6:8*.

REMARRIAGE

Divorced people—*Deuteronomy 24:1-4*.

Paul's instructions—*Romans 7:1-3*.

Widows—*1 Corinthians 7:8,9; 1 Timothy 5:11*.

REMORSE

Broken heart—*Lamentations 1:20*.

God heals the brokenhearted—*Psalm 147:3*.

Humble and contrite—*Isaiah 66:2; 1 Peter 5:5*.

Impenitent have no remorse—*Jeremiah 44:10*.

Prayer of remorse—*Psalm 51*.

REPENTANCE

Be humble and repent—*2 Chronicles 7:14*.

Confess and find mercy—*Proverbs 28:13.*
God commands repentance—*Acts 17:30.*
God desires all to repent—*2 Peter 3:9.*
Godly sorrow brings repentance—*2 Corinthians 7:10.*
Produce fruit of repentance—*Matthew 3:8.*
Prove repentance by deeds—*Acts 26:20.*
Repent and turn to God—*Acts 3:19.*
Return to God with whole heart—*Joel 2:12,13.*
Unless you repent, you perish—*Luke 13:3.*

REPROOF

Do not bother rebuking mockers—*Proverbs 9:8.*
Do not ignore criticism—*Proverbs 13:18.*
Listen to constructive criticism—*Proverbs 15:31.*
Open rebuke better than hidden love—*Proverbs 27:5.*
Patiently correct, rebuke—*2 Timothy 4:2.*
Privately point out person's fault—*Matthew 18:15.*
Reject criticism, harm only yourself—*Proverbs 15:32.*
Speak truth in love—*Ephesians 4:15.*
Warn each other—*Hebrews 3:13.*
Whoever hates correction will die—*Proverbs 15:10.*
Wound from friend better—*Proverbs 27:6.*

REPUTATION, GOOD

Choose a good reputation—*Proverbs 22:1.*
Good reputation is valuable—*Ecclesiastes 7:1.*

RESENTMENT

Godless harbor resentment—*Job 36:13.*
Love covers all offenses—*Proverbs 10:12.*
Mocker resents correction—*Proverbs 15:12.*

Prodigal son's brother—*Luke 15:11-32.*

Resentment kills a fool—*Job 5:2.*

RESPECT

Live so others respect you—*1 Thessalonians 4:12.*

Respect aged people—*Leviticus 19:32; Job 32:6.*

Respect church leadership—*Philippians 2:29.*

Respect parents—*Leviticus 19:3; Ephesians 6:1,2.*

Respect Scripture—*Nehemiah 8:5.*

Wives must be respected—*1 Timothy 3:11.*

Wives respect husbands—*Ephesians 5:33.*

RESPONSIBILITY

Individual responsibility—*Ezekiel 18:20.*

Manual of responsible living—*Book of Proverbs.*

Responsible for words spoken—*Matthew 12:36,37.*

Responsible to God—*Ezekiel 18:20; Romans 3:19.*

Trustworthy people, more responsibility—*Luke 16:10.*

Wife is responsible to husband—*1 Corinthians 11:3.*

REST

Jesus and disciples rested—*Mark 6:31.*

Jesus rested in midst of storm—*Matthew 8:24.*

Rest on seventh day—*Exodus 23:12; 34:21.*

Spiritual

Enter God's place of rest—*Hebrews 4:1.*

Find rest in God—*Psalm 62:1.*

God gives rest to the weary—*Jeremiah 31:25.*

You will find rest for your souls—*Matthew 11:28,29.*

RESTITUTION

Compensate for loss of life—*Exodus 21:30.*

Compensate for stolen animals—*Leviticus 24:18.*
Compensate for stolen goods—*Exodus 22:1.*
Make full restitution—*Numbers 5:7.*

RESTORATION, FINAL

Final restoration of all things—*Acts 3:21.*
New heaven and new earth—*Revelation 21:1.*

RESURRECTION

Believers will be resurrected—*John 6:39,40,44,54.*
Dead will hear Christ's voice—*John 5:25,28,29.*
Eternal body made for us by God—*2 Corinthians 5:1.*
Glorious bodies—*Philippians 3:21.*
If Christ not raised, faith vain—*1 Corinthians 15:12-21.*
Jesus is the resurrection and the life—*John 11:24,25.*
Perishable becomes imperishable—*1 Corinthians 15:42.*
Resurrection of righteous and wicked—*Acts 24:15.*
Resurrection will swallow up death—*Isaiah 25:8.*
We will all be changed—*1 Corinthians 15:50-52.*

REVELATION

General revelation found in creation—*Psalm 19:1-4.*
God is revealed in His provisions for man—*Acts 14:17.*
God is the source of revelation—*Hebrews 1:1,2.*
God reveals more to those who seek Him—*Acts 10:1-31; Hebrews 11:6.*
Special revelation in Jesus—*Hebrews 1:2.*

REVENGE

Do not repay evil for evil—*1 Thessalonians 5:15.*
God will avenge—*Deuteronomy 32:43; Psalm 9:12.*
Never avenge yourselves—*Romans 12:17,19.*
Vengeance is God's—*Psalm 94:1.*

REVERENCE TO GOD

Be sure to fear the Lord—*1 Samuel 12:24.*
Live in the fear of the Lord—*Acts 9:31.*
Worship God with reverence—*Hebrews 12:28.*

REVIVAL

Day of Pentecost—*Acts 2:1-42,46,47.*
God renews hearts—*Ezekiel 11:19.*
Pray for—*Habakkuk 3:2.*
Restoration—*Hosea 6:2.*
Return to the Lord—*Lamentations 3:40.*

REWARD

Do good in secret, God will reward—*Matthew 6:1-6.*
Eternal rewards—*1 Corinthians 3:5-10.*
God rewards based on deeds—*Revelation 22:12.*
God rewards those who seek Him—*Hebrews 11:6.*
Good will be rewarded—*Ephesians 6:8.*
Great is your reward in heaven—*Matthew 5:12.*
Inheritance as a reward—*Colossians 3:24.*
Rewarded with long life—*Exodus 20:12.*
Righteous are rewarded—*Psalm 58:11.*

RICHES

Better to be poor and godly—*Proverbs 16:8.*
Better to have little with fear—*Proverbs 15:16.*
Blessing of Lord makes person rich—*Proverbs 10:22.*
Do not store up treasures on earth—*Matthew 6:19.*
Greedy person tries to get rich quick—*Proverbs 28:22.*
Lord makes one poor and another rich—*1 Samuel 2:7.*
Lure of wealth—*Mark 4:19.*

Riches do not last—*Proverbs 27:24*.

Riches no help on judgment day—*Proverbs 11:4*.

RIGHTEOUSNESS

Abraham believed, righteous—*Genesis 15:6*.

Eyes of Lord are on the righteous—*Psalm 34:15*.

Lord hears prayers of righteous—*Proverbs 15:28,29*.

No one righteous by obeying law—*Romans 3:10-20*.

Prayer of righteous man is effective—*James 5:16*.

Righteous will live by faith—*Romans 1:17*.

RISING

Early

Do not get up early to do evil—*Micah 2:1*.

Do not get up early to drink—*Isaiah 5:11*.

Jesus' example, early devotions—*Mark 1:35*.

New strength every morning—*Isaiah 33:2*.

Prayer in the morning—*Psalm 5:3; 119:147*.

Late

A little extra sleep leads to poverty—*Proverbs 24:33,34*.

Lazybones, how long will you sleep?—*Proverbs 6:9*.

Love sleep, end in poverty—*Proverbs 20:13*.

ROBBERY

Do not steal—*Exodus 20:15; Leviticus 19:11*.

If you are a thief, stop stealing—*Ephesians 4:28*.

Lord hates robbery—*Isaiah 61:8*.

Robbing the poor is wrong—*Amos 8:4*.

RULERS, WICKED

Destruction certain for unjust judges—*Isaiah 10:1.*
Officials and judges alike demand bribes—*Micah 7:3.*
Rebellious leaders—*Isaiah 1:23.*
Some leaders are like wolves—*Ezekiel 22:27.*
Wicked ruler is dangerous—*Proverbs 28:15.*
Wicked rulers ruined Israel—*Isaiah 3:14.*

SABBATH

Day of rest—*Exodus 16:23*.
Do not let anyone judge you—*Colossians 2:16*.
God rested seventh day—*Genesis 2:2,3*.
Lord of the Sabbath—*Matthew 12:8*.
Sabbath-rest—*Hebrews 4:9*.

SACRIFICE

Body is a living sacrifice—*Romans 12:1*.
Christ our example—*1 John 3:16*.
Christ, the ultimate sacrifice—*Hebrews 10:1-10*.
Obedience is better than sacrifice—*1 Samuel 15:22*.
Old Testament sacrifices pointed to Christ's—*Ephesians 5:2; Hebrews 10:1*.
Sacrifice cannot take away sin—*Hebrews 9:9; 10:1-11*.
Sacrifice of praise—*Hebrews 13:15*.
Sacrifice of thanksgiving—*Psalm 116:17*.

SADDUCEES

Beware of their yeast—*Matthew 16:6*.
Brood of snakes—*Matthew 3:7*.
Denied belief in resurrection—*Matthew 22:23*.

SAFETY

Daniel protected in lion's den—*Daniel 6:13-24*.
Go your way in safety—*Proverbs 3:23*.
God is our shield—*Deuteronomy 33:29*.
God will not let your foot slip—*Psalm 121:3*.
God's people live securely—*Isaiah 32:18*.

SALVATION

Adoption into God's family—*Galatians 4:5.*
Believe and be saved—*John 3:14-17; 5:24; 6:29,47.*
By grace through faith—*Ephesians 2:8,9.*
Imputation of righteousness—*Romans 4:5.*
Jesus died in our place—*Matthew 20:28.*
Justification—*Romans 3:28; 5:1,2,9.*
New birth—*John 3:3.*
Propitiation—*1 John 2:2.*
Reconciliation to God—*2 Corinthians 5:18.*
Redemption—*2 Peter 2:1.*
Salvation only in Christ—*John 14:16; Acts 4:12.*
Sanctification—*1 Corinthians 6:11.*
Sins become white as snow—*Isaiah 1:18.*
Works not involved—*Romans 11:6.*

SANCTIFICATION

Avoid sexual immorality—*1 Thessalonians 4:3.*
Positional sanctification—*1 Corinthians 6:11.*
Sanctified by faith—*Acts 26:17,18.*
Sanctified by truth—*John 17:17,19.*
Sanctified in Christ—*1 Corinthians 1:2.*
Sanctified through and through—*1 Thessalonians 5:23.*
Sanctifying work of the Holy Spirit—*1 Peter 1:1,2.*

SANITATION

Disinfection

After childbirth—*Leviticus 12:2-5; Ezekiel 16:4.*
After touching dead animals—*Leviticus 11:24-40.*
Burn unclean things—*Leviticus 7:19.*
Cleansing ceremony—*Leviticus 14:8,9.*
Related to disease—*Leviticus 15.*

Food

Do not eat blood—*Leviticus 19:26; Deuteronomy 12:16.*

Do not eat unclean animals—*Leviticus 11:26,27,29.*

Meat to be eaten same day offered—*Leviticus 7:15.*

Never eat fat—*Leviticus 7:23.*

Quarantine

Call out, "Unclean! Unclean!"—*Leviticus 13:45.*

Infection, quarantine—*Leviticus 13:31.*

Keep a distance—*Luke 17:12.*

Live in isolation—*Leviticus 13:46.*

Live outside camp—*Leviticus 14:3; Numbers 5:2.*

SATAN

Accuses and slanders believers— *Revelation 12:10.*

Deceives whole world—*Revelation 12:9.*

Fatherhood of the devil—*John 8:44.*

Fosters spiritual pride—*1 Timothy 3:6.*

God of this evil world—*2 Corinthians 4:4.*

Has followers—*1 Timothy 5:15.*

Hinders answers to prayers—*Daniel 10:12-20.*

Instigates jealousy—*James 3:13-16.*

Is a cherub—*Ezekiel 28:14.*

Liar and murderer—*John 8:44.*

Lucifer (Satan) rebelled against God—*Isaiah 14:12-15.*

Masquerades as angel of light—*2 Corinthians 11:14.*

Plants doubt in minds of believers—*Genesis 3:1-5.*

Prowls like roaring lion—*1 Peter 5:8.*

Resist the devil—*James 4:7.*

Satanic possession—*Mark 3:22.*

Synagogue of Satan—*Revelation 2:9.*

Tempts believers to immorality—*1 Corinthians 7:5.*
Tempts believers to lie—*Acts 5:3.*
Wear spiritual armor—*Ephesians 6:11-18.*

SCOFFING

Avoid scoffers—*Psalm 1:1.*
Enemies continually taunt—*Psalm 42:3.*
Mocker refuses to listen—*Proverbs 13:1.*
Mockers are proud and haughty—*Proverbs 21:24.*
Mockers will be punished—*Proverbs 19:29.*
Scoffers in the last days—*2 Peter 3:3,4.*
Scoffing at the Almighty—*Job 21:15.*

SCRIPTURE

Inerrancy of

All God's words are true—*Psalm 119:160.*
Every jot and tittle accurate—*Matthew 5:17,18.*
Every word of God is flawless—*Proverbs 30:5,6.*
God's commands are true—*Psalm 119:151.*
God's word is truth—*John 17:17.*
God's words are flawless—*Psalm 12:6; 18:30.*
Law of Lord is perfect—*Psalm 19:7.*
Letters of words accurate—*Matthew 22:41-46.*
Scripture cannot be broken—*John 10:35.*
Singular word is accurate—*Galatians 3:16.*
Verb tense accurate—*Matthew 22:23-33.*

Inspiration of

All Scripture is inspired—*2 Timothy 3:16.*
Christ spoke through Paul—*2 Corinthians 13:2,3.*
God put His words in Jeremiah's mouth—*Jeremiah 1:9.*

God taught Moses what to speak—*Exodus 4:12-16.*
Holy Spirit guided apostles into truth—*John 14:26.*
Holy Spirit moved biblical writers—*2 Peter 1:21.*
Holy Spirit spoke through David—*2 Samuel 23:2,3.*
Jeremiah wrote God's words—*Jeremiah 30:1,2.*
Luke's Gospel recognized as Scripture—*1 Timothy 5:18.*
Paul wrote at Lord's command—*1 Corinthians 14:37.*
Paul's words were God's words—*1 Thessalonians 2:13.*
Paul's writings recognized as Scripture—*2 Peter 3:16.*
Scripture cannot be broken—*John 10:35.*
Words "taught" by Holy Spirit—*1 Corinthians 2:13.*

SECOND COMING OF CHRIST

Be blameless until He comes—*1 Thessalonians 5:23.*
Be patient as you await Lord's return—*James 5:7.*
Christ will come like a thief—*1 Thessalonians 5:1-3.*
Christ will come visibly—*Acts 1:9-11.*
Coming from heaven—*1 Thessalonians 1:10.*
Coming soon—*Philippians 4:5; Revelation 22:12,20.*
Every eye will see Him—*Revelation 1:7.*
No one knows hour—*Matthew 24:42,44,46-50.*
Return of our Lord Jesus—*1 Corinthians 1:7,8.*
Scoffers in the last days—*2 Peter 3:4.*
Signs in the sun, moon, and stars—*Luke 21:25,27.*
We eagerly wait—*Philippians 3:20; Titus 2:13.*
Will bring us to place He prepared—*John 14:3.*
Will come back on clouds of heaven—*Matthew 26:64.*
Will come in glory—*Matthew 16:27; 25:31; Mark 8:38.*

SECRECY

Confront secretly—*Matthew 18:15.*

Discuss privately—*Proverbs 25:9*.

Give secretly—*Matthew 6:4*.

Pray secretly—*Matthew 6:6*.

SECURITY, FALSE

Long, good life assured?—*Job 29:18*.

People think God does not care what they do—*Psalm 50:21*.

People think they are safe—*Jeremiah 21:13*.

People trust in wealth—*Jeremiah 49:4*.

Sudden death—*Amos 9:10*.

When crime not punished, people do wrong—*Ecclesiastes 8:11*.

Wicked people think God is dead—*Psalm 10:4*.

SEDUCTION

Joseph flees from—*Genesis 39:6-20*.

Seduced away from the faith—*1 Timothy 4:1*.

Seductive woman—*Proverbs 7:6-27; Ecclesiastes 7:26*.

SELF-CONDEMNATION

David recognized his sin—*2 Samuel 24:17*.

Job's own mouth pronounced him guilty—*Job 9:20*.

"Why didn't I listen?"—*Proverbs 5:13*.

SELF-CONTROL

Control tongue and live long—*Proverbs 13:3*.

Do not let sin control you—*Romans 6:12*.

Exhibit self-control—*1 Timothy 3:2; Titus 2:2*.

Fruit of the spirit—*Galatians 5:22,23*.

Great value in controlling temper—*Proverbs 16:32*.

Reward of self-control—*Revelation 21:7*.

Self-control over life in general—*Acts 24:25*.

Self-Denial

Avoid shameful desires—*Colossians 3:5; 1 Peter 2:11*.

Do not be tied up in affairs of life—*2 Timothy 2:4*.

Do not hold on to rights—*1 Corinthians 9:12-25*.

Do not indulge evil desires—*Romans 13:14*.

Do not let eye cause you to sin—*Matthew 5:29,30*.

Do not let hand cause you to sin—*Mark 9:43*.

Do not think only of your good—*1 Corinthians 10:24*.

Give up your life for Jesus—*Matthew 16:24,25*.

Go and sell all you have—*Matthew 19:21*.

Leave everything to follow Jesus—*Luke 5:11*.

Put aside selfish ambition—*Mark 8:34; Luke 9:23*.

Self-Examination

Examine yourself—*1 Corinthians 11:28,31*.

Lord, show me what offends—*Psalm 139:24*.

Lord, search me—*Psalm 139:23*.

Lord, show me my rebellion—*Job 13:23*.

Lord, test my motives—*Psalm 26:2*.

Selfishness

Do not just please yourself—*2 Corinthians 5:15*.

Do not think only about your affairs—*Philippians 2:4*.

Do not think only of your good—*1 Corinthians 10:24*.

Share each other's troubles—*Galatians 6:2*.

Self-Pity

Cure for self-pity—*Psalm 37*.

Turn from self-pity—*Proverbs 15:13*.

Self-Righteous

Empty claim of no sin—*Jeremiah 2:35*.

Get rid of log from own eye—*Matthew 7:5.*
God detests—*Isaiah 65:5.*
Holier than thou—*Luke 18:9.*
Hypocrites call on Lord but will not obey—*Luke 6:46.*
Hypocrites clean outside, filthy inside—*Luke 11:39.*
Jesus speaks against—*Matthew 23:27,28.*

SERVANT, BOND

Be a faithful servant—*Matthew 25:23.*
Better to be a servant than ambitious—*Luke 22:26.*
Lord will reward—*Ephesians 6:8.*
No slave or free in Christ—*Galatians 3:28.*
Paul became a servant of everyone—*1 Corinthians 9:19.*
Servant leaders—*Matthew 20:28; Mark 10:43,44.*

SEX WITHIN MARRIAGE

Marriage bed should be honored by all—*Hebrews 13:4.*
Sex within marriage good—*Matthew 19:5.*
Two become one flesh—*Matthew 19:5; Mark 10:7,8.*

SEXUAL ABERRATIONS

Avoid people who indulge in sexual sin—*1 Corinthians 5:9.*
Body not made for sexual immorality—*1 Corinthians 6:13.*
Homosexuality—*Leviticus 18:22.*
Immoral lives—*Jude 4.*
Keep clear of sexual sin—*Colossians 3:5.*
No immoral living—*Romans 13:13.*
No sex with close relative—*Leviticus 18:6.*
No sex with neighbor's wife—*Leviticus 18:20.*
Sexual immorality brings judgment—*1 Corinthians 10:8.*

Sexual immorality calls for discipline—*1 Corinthians 5:1-11.*

Sexual immorality emerges from sinful nature—*Galatians 5:19.*

SHAME

Adam and Eve naked, felt no shame—*Genesis 2:25.*

After sin, Adam and Eve felt shame—*Genesis 3:7.*

Avoid shameful desires—*Colossians 3:5; 1 Peter 2:11.*

Fool is put to shame—*Proverbs 3:35.*

Lord, do not let me be put to shame—*Psalm 31:1.*

No shame to suffer as a Christian—*1 Peter 4:16.*

Pride leads to shame—*Proverbs 11:2.*

Sin leads to shame and disgrace—*Genesis 3:7.*

SHEEP, FIGURATIVE

Disciples are sheep among wolves—*Matthew 10:16.*

Israel, God's lost sheep—*Matthew 10:6.*

Sheep of flock (disciples) will be scattered—*Mark 14:27.*

Sheep without a shepherd—*Matthew 9:36.*

Straying sheep—*Luke 15:4.*

SHEPHERD, GOD IS

Carries lambs in His arms—*Isaiah 40:11.*

God leads His people like a flock—*Psalm 78:52.*

Jesus the Good Shepherd—*John 10:11.*

Jesus the great Shepherd—*Hebrews 13:20.*

Lord is my Shepherd—*Psalm 23.*

Shepherd, Guardian of your souls—*1 Peter 2:25.*

SIGN

Miraculous signs—*John 2:11; 3:2.*

"Show us a miraculous sign"—*Matthew 12:38*.
Sign of coming of Son of Man—*Matthew 24:3,30*.
Signs of the times—*Matthew 16:3,4*.

SIN

All humans have sinned—*Isaiah 53:5-6; Romans 3:23*.
Devastating effects of sin—*Romans 1:18–3:20*.
Fallen man is totally depraved—*Romans 7:18*.
God chastens us if we remain in sin—*Hebrews 12:6*.
God's Word in our hearts prevents sin—
    Psalm 119:11.
Sin breaks our fellowship with God—*Isaiah 59:1,2*.
Sin causes death—*Romans 6:23*.
Sin is lawlessness—*1 John 3:4*.
Sin unto death—*1 Corinthians 11:30; 1 John 5:16*.
Three areas of sin: lust of flesh, lust of eyes, pride of
    life—*1 John 2:16*.
We are sinful from moment of birth—*Psalm 51:5*.

Against Holy Spirit

Blasphemy against the Holy Spirit—*Matthew 12:31,32*.
Grieve the Holy Spirit—*Isaiah 63:10; Ephesians 4:30*.
Lie to the Holy Spirit—*Acts 5:3*.
Resist the Holy Spirit—*Acts 7:51*.

Confession of

Confess sins to each other—*James 5:16*.
Confess your sins—*1 John 1:9*.
Confession cleanses guilt away—*Psalm 51:2*.
Confession leads to healing—*Psalm 41:4*.
Model prayer of confession—*Psalm 51*.

Consequences of

Destruction—*Proverbs 13:6*.

Enslavement to sinful desires—*1 Corinthians 3:3*.

Entraps us—*Psalm 9:16; Proverbs 12:13; 29:6*.

Fall into own snares—*Psalm 141:10*.

Full of trouble—*Proverbs 12:21*.

Held captive by sins—*Proverbs 5:22*.

No peace—*Isaiah 57:21*.

Separates us from God—*Ephesians 4:17-19*.

Shame and disgrace—*Genesis 3:7; Proverbs 3:35; 13:5*.

Ultimately leads to death—*Romans 5:12; 6:23*.

We do what we do not want to do—*Romans 7:14,15*.

Forgiveness of

Cleansing from every sin—*1 John 1:7*.

Forgiveness and cleansing—*1 John 1:9*.

God blots out sins—*Isaiah 43:25,26*.

God forgives *all* our sins—*Psalm 65:3; 99:8; Luke 5:21*.

Guilt removed—*Psalm 32:5*.

Jesus saves His people from sins—*Matthew 1:21*.

Joy for those whose rebellion is forgiven—*Psalm 32:1,2*.

Known to God

God carefully watches how people live—*Job 24:23*.

God knows secrets of every heart—*Psalm 44:21*.

God sees every sin—*Jeremiah 16:17; Hosea 7:2*.

God sees secret sins—*Psalm 90:8*.

Love of

✗ Dog returns to its vomit—*Proverbs 26:11*.

Enjoying evil—*Proverbs 2:14*.

Enjoying the taste of wickedness—*Job 20:12*.

Separates from God

God hides His face—*Deuteronomy 31:18*.

Sins cut us off from God—*Isaiah 59:2*.

SINCERITY

Be completely honest—*Psalm 32:2*.

Be honest and sincere—*2 Corinthians 1:12*.

Do not just pretend to be good—*1 Peter 2:1*.

Do not just pretend to love others—*Romans 12:9*.

SINLESSNESS

Be blameless—*1 Thessalonians 3:13*.

Be holy in every way—*1 Thessalonians 5:23*.

Do not compromise—*Psalm 119:3*.

No one is absolutely sinless—*1 John 1:10*.

SKEPTICISM

Doubtful mind is unsettled—*James 1:6*.

Fools deny God's existence—*Psalm 14:1; 53:1*.

Satan plants doubt in minds—*Genesis 3:1-5*.

Skepticism about prayer—*Job 21:15*.

Waver back and forth—*1 Kings 18:21; James 1:8*.

SLANDER

Avoid rumors—*Psalm 31:13*.

Do not speak evil of anyone—*1 Timothy 3:11; Titus 3:2*.

False accusations—*Psalm 35:11*.

False witness—*Matthew 26:60*.

Get rid of slander—*Ephesians 4:31*.

Keep your tongue from speaking evil—*1 Peter 3:10*.

Slander and telling lies—*Psalm 109:2*.

Will answer for every idle word—*Matthew 12:36*.

SLAVERY

Be slaves of righteousness—*Romans 6:19*.
Enslaved to sin—*John 8:34; Romans 6:16*.
No slave or free in Christ—*Galatians 3:28*.
Slaves of God—*Romans 6:22*.
Slaves to evil pleasures—*Titus 3:3*.

SLEEP

Girl slept in death—*Matthew 9:24; Mark 5:39*.
God gives rest to His loved ones—*Psalm 127:2*.
Lazybones, how long will you sleep?—*Proverbs 6:9*.

SOBRIETY

Be sober—*1 Thessalonians 5:6*.
Do not be heavy drinker—*1 Timothy 3:3*.
Exhibit self-control—*1 Timothy 3:2; Titus 2:2*.
Live soberly—*Titus 2:12*.

SODOMY

Burn with lust—*Romans 1:27*.
Do not practice homosexuality—*Genesis 19:5-7*.
Homosexuals no share in Kingdom—*1 Corinthians 6:9*.
Penalty for homosexual acts—*Leviticus 20:13*.
Turning against natural feelings—*Romans 1:26*.

SON

Abraham willing to sacrifice son—*Genesis 22:1-18*.
Dedicate firstborn sons to God—*Exodus 13:2,12,13,15*.
Lord killed firstborn sons in Egypt—*Exodus 12:29*.
Prodigal son—*Luke 15:11-32*.
Redemption of firstborn sons—*Exodus 22:29,30*.

Son listen to father—*Proverbs 1:8; 13:1*.

Son who sleeps during harvest, shameful—*Proverbs 10:5*.

SONG

God has given us a new song—*Psalm 40:3*.

Great choir sang wonderful new song—*Revelation 14:3*.

Moses and people sang to Lord—*Exodus 15:1*.

Psalms, hymns, and spiritual songs—*Ephesians 5:19*.

Sing new songs of praise—*Psalm 33:3*.

SORROW

Do not sorrow over dead in Christ—*1 Thessalonians 4:13*.

God will wipe away all tears—*Revelation 21:4*.

Godly sorrow produces good—*2 Corinthians 7:10,11*.

Sorrowful, yet rejoicing—*2 Corinthians 6:10*.

SPEAKING

Evil

Avoid foul or abusive language—*Romans 3:13,14*.

Avoid perverse talk—*Proverbs 4:24*.

Deceitful tongue crushes spirit—*Proverbs 15:4*.

Do not speak evil—*James 4:11; 1 Peter 3:10*.

False witness tells lies—*Proverbs 12:17*.

Gossiping tongue causes anger—*Proverbs 25:23*.

Harsh words stir up anger—*Proverbs 15:1*.

Just say *yes* or *no*—*Matthew 5:37*.

Keep your lips from telling lies—*Psalm 34:13*.

No one can tame tongue—*James 3:8*.

Obscene stories and coarse jokes—*Ephesians 5:4*.

Quick retort can ruin everything—*Proverbs 13:3*.

Tongue can cut like sharp razor—*Psalm 52:2*.

Tongue can do enormous damage—*James 3:5*.

Tongue can sting like a snake—*Psalm 140:3.*
Wicked are trapped by their words—*Proverbs 12:13.*

Wisdom in

Be slow to speak—*James 1:19.*
Control tongue and live long—*Proverbs 13:3.*
Curb your tongue—*Psalm 39:1.*
Do not brag—*James 3:13.*
Do not let lips speak evil—*Job 27:4.*
Gentle answer turns away wrath—*Proverbs 15:1.*
Gentle words bring life and health—*Proverbs 15:4.*
Good words come from good heart—*Matthew 12:35.*
Let conversation be gracious—*Colossians 4:6.*
Let Lord control what you say—*Psalm 141:3.*
Lord delights in pure words—*Proverbs 15:26.*
Soft speech crushes opposition—*Proverbs 25:15.*
Speak encouraging words—*Ephesians 4:29.*
Wise person uses few words—*Proverbs 17:27.*
Words of wise keep them out of trouble—*Proverbs 14:3.*

SPIRITUALITY, PRINCIPLES OF

Bow down in worship—*Psalm 95:6.*
Fix thoughts on God—*Isaiah 26:3.*
Holy Spirit guides us—*John 14:17.*
Let Word of God guide you—*Psalm 119:105.*
Love Lord with whole heart—*Deuteronomy 6:5.*
Obey all commands—*Joshua 22:5.*
Set sights on heaven—*Colossians 3:1.*
Trust in God completely—*Proverbs 3:5,6.*

STARS

Do not worship stars—*Deuteronomy 4:19.*

God commands stars—*Job 9:7*.
God made the stars—*Genesis 1:16; Job 9:9*.
God set the stars in place—*Psalm 8:3*.
God spoke, and the stars were born—*Psalm 33:6*.

STEALING

Do not steal—*Exodus 20:15; Leviticus 19:11*.
If you are a thief, stop stealing—*Ephesians 4:28*.
Store treasure in heaven, where it cannot be
  stolen—*Matthew 6:19,20*.

STRENGTH, GOD IS OUR

Can do all things through Christ—*Philippians 4:13*.
God gives power to the faint—*Isaiah 40:29,31*.
God will strengthen you—*Psalm 27:14; Isaiah 41:10*.
God's grace is sufficient—*2 Corinthians 12:9*.

STRIFE

Aim for harmony—*Romans 14:19*.
Contentious wife—*Proverbs 19:13; 21:19; 25:24;
  27:15*.
Fools insist on quarreling—*Proverbs 20:3*.
Quarreling, jealousy, anger—*2 Corinthians 12:20*.
Stay away from arguing—*Philippians 2:14*.
Stay free from anger and controversy—*1 Timothy 2:8*.
Stop arguing—*1 Corinthians 1:10*.

STUDENTS

Holy Spirit is our teacher—*1 Corinthians 2:6-16*.
Learn about God and His ways—*Deuteronomy 4:10*.
Learn Scriptures from childhood—*2 Timothy 3:15*.
Study the Bible—*Deuteronomy 17:19; Isaiah 34:16*.

SUBMISSION

Be careful to obey God—*Exodus 19:5; 23:22*.

Obey leaders and submit to them—*Hebrews 13:17*.

Submit to God—*James 4:7*.

Submit to government—*Titus 3:1*.

Submit to those who are older—*1 Peter 5:5*.

Wives submit to husbands—*Ephesians 5:22-24*.

SUCCESS

God of heaven gives success—*Nehemiah 2:20*.

Hard work means prosperity—*Proverbs 12:11*.

Many counselors bring success—*Proverbs 15:22*.

Observe laws, then will prosper—*1 Chronicles 22:13*.

Seek first the Kingdom—*Matthew 6:33*.

Seek Lord and succeed—*2 Chronicles 26:5*.

Whatever godly person does prospers—*Psalm 1:3*.

SUFFERING

Blessed are those who suffer for doing right—*1 Peter 3:14-17*.

Christ is our example in suffering—*1 Peter 2:21*.

Christ's consolation is abundant—*2 Corinthians 1:5*.

No trouble can separate us from Christ—*Romans 8:35*.

Rejoice in midst of fiery trials—*1 Peter 4:12,13*.

Rejoice in suffering—*Romans 5:3*.

Suffering not comparable to future glory—*Romans 8:18*.

SUICIDE

Assisted suicide—*Jonah 1:12 (see 1 Samuel 31:4)*.

Judas's suicide—*Matthew 27:5; Acts 1:18*.

Pigs committed pigicide—*Luke 8:26-34*.

Saul's suicide—*1 Samuel 31:4*.

Suicide refused—*1 Samuel 31:4; 1 Chronicles 10:4*.

SUN

Do not worship sun—*Deuteronomy 17:3.*
God separated day from night—*Genesis 1:14.*
Sun stood still—*Joshua 10:12,13.*
Sun will become dark—*Matthew 24:29; Mark 13:24.*

SYMPATHY

Be full of sympathy toward each other—*1 Peter 3:8.*
Be Good Samaritan—*Luke 10:30-37.*
Bear each other's burdens—*Galatians 6:2; Hebrews 13:3.*
Do not just pretend to love others—*Romans 12:9,10.*
Love your neighbor as yourself—*Leviticus 19:18.*

TABERNACLE

Made according to God's design—*Exodus 26:30*.

Residence built for God—*Exodus 25:8*.

TACT

Gentle answer turns away wrath—*Proverbs 15:1*.

Paul became servant of everyone—*1 Corinthians 9:19*.

Soft speech can crush opposition—*Proverbs 25:15*.

Speak truth in love—*Ephesians 4:15*.

TAX

Annual temple tax—*Nehemiah 10:32*.

Borrow to pay taxes—*Nehemiah 5:4*.

Collectors, collect only amount owed—*Luke 3:13*.

In proportion to wealth—*2 Kings 23:35*.

Jesus and the temple tax—*Matthew 17:24*.

Jesus associated with tax collectors—*Matthew 11:19*.

TEACHERS, FALSE

Do not teach others to break God's law—*Matthew 5:19*.

False prophets deceive—*Matthew 7:15; 24:11*.

False teachers deceive—*Matthew 5:19*.

TEACHING

Fear of Lord teaches person to be wise—*Proverbs 15:33*.

Fool ignores Christ's teaching—*Matthew 7:26*.

God gives teachers to the church—*Ephesians 4:11*.

Hold on to pattern of right teaching—*2 Timothy 1:13*.

Holy Spirit teaches believers—*John 16:13-15*.

Impress God's Word on children—*Deuteronomy 6:7*.

Listen to what parents teach—*Proverbs 1:8; 6:20; 23:22.*
People will turn from right teaching—*2 Timothy 4:3.*

Tears

God collects our tears in bottle—*Psalm 56:8.*
God will wipe away all tears—*Revelation 7:17.*
No more sorrow or crying or pain—*Revelation 21:4.*

Teeth

Enemies grind their teeth—*Lamentations 2:16.*
Evil spirit caused grinding teeth—*Mark 9:18.*
Weeping and gnashing of teeth—*Matthew 8:12.*

Temperance

Deacon, not heavy drinker—*1 Timothy 3:8.*
Elder, not heavy drinker—*1 Timothy 3:3; Titus 1:7.*
Older women, not heavy drinkers—*Titus 2:3.*

Temple

Ark brought to temple—*1 Kings 8:1-21.*
Dedication of temple—*2 Chronicles 7:1-10.*
Gifts for building temple—*1 Chronicles 29:1-9.*
Glory of Lord in temple—*Ezekiel 10:4.*
Moneychangers in temple—*John 2:14-16.*
Prediction of destruction—*Matthew 24:2; Mark 13:2.*
Preparations for temple—*1 Chronicles 22:2-19.*
Temple furnishings—*1 Kings 7:13-51; 2 Chronicles 4.*

Temptation

Beware of temptations—*Galatians 6:1.*
Do not let evil get best of you—*Romans 12:21.*
Do not let Satan outsmart you—*2 Corinthians 2:11.*
Do not let sin control you—*Romans 6:12.*

Do not lose secure footing—*2 Peter 3:17*.

God can keep you from falling—*Jude 24*.

God will make way of escape—*1 Corinthians 10:13*.

Jesus helps us in our temptation—*Hebrews 2:14,18*.

Keep alert and pray—*Matthew 26:41; Mark 14:38*.

Lord, do not let us yield—*Matthew 6:9-13*.

Pray that you will not be overcome—*Luke 22:40*.

Resist the devil—*James 4:7*.

Satan tempts sexually—*1 Corinthians 7:5*.

Temptations emerge from sin nature—*James 1:13-15*.

Three kinds of temptations—*1 John 2:16*.

Watch out for temptation of money—*1 Timothy 6:9*.

TENSION, CURE FOR

Let not your heart be troubled—*John 14:27*.

Mind stayed on God is in perfect peace—*Isaiah 26:3*.

Peace and joy in the Holy Spirit—*Romans 14:17*.

Peace of God guards your heart—*Philippians 4:7*.

TESTIFY ON GOD'S BEHALF

Acknowledge Christ publicly—*Matthew 10:32*.

Be ready with an answer—*1 Peter 3:15*.

Confess with your mouth—*Romans 10:9*.

Never be ashamed to tell others—*2 Timothy 1:8*.

Tell family—*Luke 8:39*.

Tell friends—*Mark 5:19*.

Witnesses to the ends of the earth—*Acts 1:8*.

THANKFULNESS

Always give thanks—*Ephesians 5:20; Colossians 3:15*.

Come before God with thanksgiving—*Psalm 95:2*.

Give thanks forever—*Psalm 30:12*.

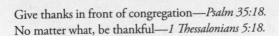

Give thanks in front of congregation—*Psalm 35:18*.
No matter what, be thankful—*1 Thessalonians 5:18*.

THANKSGIVING BEFORE MEALS

Give thanks to God before eating—*Romans 14:6*.
Jesus our example—*Matthew 14:19; 15:36; 26:26*.

THEFT AND THIEVES

Do not cheat or rob anyone—*Leviticus 19:11,13*.
Do not steal—*Exodus 20:15; Deuteronomy 5:19*.
From the heart comes theft—*Matthew 15:19*.
God hates robbery—*Isaiah 61:8*.

THIRST

As deer pants, so psalmist thirsts for God—*Psalm 42:1*.
If you are thirsty, come to Christ—*John 7:37*.
Let the thirsty ones come—*Revelation 22:17*.
To the thirsty Jesus gives water of life—*Revelation 21:6*.

THRONE, EXAMPLES OF

Father acknowledges Jesus' eternal throne—*Hebrews 1:8*.
Isaiah sees God on throne—*Isaiah 6:1-5*.
Jesus reigns on throne of David—*Psalm 132:11*.
Throne of God in heaven—*Revelation 4:2-6,9,10*.

TIME

Christ created "the ages"—*Hebrews 1:2*.
Day is like thousand years to the Lord—*2 Peter 3:8*.
God set boundaries for day and night—*Job 26:10*.
In the beginning God created—*Genesis 1:1*.

TITHES

A tenth of everything—*Genesis 28:22*.

Bring tithes into storehouse—*Malachi 3:10.*

Set aside a tithe of your crops—*Leviticus 27:30.*

TOLERANCE

Intolerance of disciples—*Mark 9:38,39; Luke 9:49,50.*

Jesus tolerated tax collectors—*Matthew 9:10.*

Paul's tolerance of self-serving preachers—*Philippians 1:17,18.*

Tolerance for opinions of others—*Romans 14:1-8.*

TONGUE

A time to be quiet—*Ecclesiastes 3:7.*

Do not talk too much—*Proverbs 10:19.*

Guarding mouth averts calamity—*Proverbs 21:23.*

Keep tight rein on tongue—*James 1:26.*

Keep tongue from evil—*1 Peter 3:10.*

May words be pleasing—*Psalm 19:14.*

Offer God sacrifice of praise—*Hebrews 13:15.*

Reckless words pierce soul—*Proverbs 12:18.*

Rid mouth of filthy language—*Colossians 3:8.*

Set guard at mouth—*Psalm 141:3.*

Wise person uses few words—*Proverbs 17:27.*

TRADITION

Ancient tradition—*Matthew 15:2,3; Mark 7:3.*

Human tradition—*Colossians 2:8.*

Tradition of fathers—*Galatians 1:14.*

TREASURE

Parable of the hidden treasure—*Matthew 13:44-46.*

Store treasure in heaven—*Matthew 6:19,20.*

Treasure God's words—*Job 23:12.*

We will share Christ's treasures—*Romans 8:17*.

Where your treasure is, your heart is—*Matthew 6:21*.

TRIBULATION PERIOD

Antichrist will demand worship—*2 Thessalonians 2:4*.

Events of Tribulation—*Revelation 4–18*.

Seven years long—*Daniel 9:27*.

Time of distress—*Daniel 12:1*.

Time of Jacob's distress—*Jeremiah 30:7*.

Worldwide tribulation—*Revelation 3:10*.

TROUBLE

All of us encounter trouble—*Job 5:7*.

Be patient in trouble—*Romans 12:12*.

Do not be troubled, trust Christ—*John 14:1*.

Fool invites trouble—*Proverbs 10:14*.

God helps in times of trouble—*Psalm 46:1*.

Lazy person has trouble all through life—*Proverbs 15:19*.

Let not your heart be troubled—*John 14:27*.

Lord delivers us out of trouble—*Psalm 34:17-19*.

Patiently endure troubles—*2 Corinthians 6:4*.

Present troubles insignificant in view of future glory—*2 Corinthians 4:17*.

Trust God in times of trouble—*Psalm 50:15*.

TRUSTING

Do not be troubled, trust Christ—*John 14:1*.

Do not throw away trust—*Hebrews 10:35*.

Joy in trusting God—*Psalm 40:4*.

Trust God, He will help you—*Psalm 37:5*.

Trust God in times of trouble—*Psalm 50:15*.

Trust in God at all times—*Psalm 62:8*.

Trust in Lord, not man—*Psalm 118:8*.

Trust with whole heart—*Proverbs 3:5,6*.

TRUSTWORTHY

Everything God does is worthy of trust—*Psalm 33:4*.

God guards what we entrust to Him—*2 Timothy 1:12*.

God is trustworthy—*2 Chronicles 6:4,14,15*.

Guard what God has entrusted to you—*1 Timothy 6:20*.

In God I trust—*Psalm 56:11*.

Trustworthy people given more responsibility—*Luke 16:10*.

TRUTH

Church, pillar of the truth—*1 Timothy 3:15*.

Faithfully preach truth—*2 Corinthians 6:7*.

Gently teach those who oppose truth—*2 Timothy 2:25*.

God desires truth—*Psalm 51:6*.

Honest witness tells truth—*Proverbs 12:17*.

If walk in darkness, truth not in you—*1 John 1:6,8*.

Jesus is the truth—*John 14:6*.

Live by the truth—*John 3:21*.

Set forth truth plainly—*2 Corinthians 4:2*.

Some distort the truth—*Acts 20:30*.

Speak the truth in love—*Ephesians 4:15*.

Truth will set you free—*John 8:32*.

UNBELIEF

Do not have doubtful mind—*James 1:6*.
Do not have unbelieving heart—*Hebrews 3:12*.
Impossible to please God without faith—*Hebrews 11:6*.
Unbelief at Second Coming—*Luke 18:8*.
Unbelief, despite miracles—*John 12:37*.
Unbelief in Scripture—*Luke 24:25-36*.
Unbelief, so few miracles performed—*Matthew 13:58*.

UNCERTAIN, THINGS THAT ARE

Friendship—*John 16:32*.
Future—*Proverbs 27:1*.
Life—*James 4:14*.
Riches—*Proverbs 23:5*.

UNCHARITABLE, DO NOT BE

Do not act better than everyone else—*1 Corinthians 4:7*.
Do not be judgmental—*Luke 6:37*.
Do not condemn neighbor—*James 4:12*.
Do not lack in love—*1 Corinthians 13:1*.

UNFAITHFULNESS

Covenant breakers—*Leviticus 26:15; Psalm 55:20*.
Israel's unfaithfulness—*Hosea 10:1,2*.
Marital unfaithfulness, divorce—*Matthew 5:31,32*.
Unfaithful hearts and lustful eyes—*Ezekiel 6:9*.

UNFRUITFULNESS

Fruit of the Holy Spirit—*Galatians 5:22,23.*
Fruitless deeds of darkness—*Ephesians 5:11.*
God prunes, so more fruit—*John 15:2-6.*
Good tree cannot produce bad fruit—*Luke 6:43.*
Unfruitfulness leads to judgment—*Matthew 3:10; 7:19.*

UNITY AMONG BELIEVERS

Agree wholeheartedly—*Philippians 2:2.*
Live in harmony and peace—*Romans 12:16; 14:19.*
One heart and mind—*Acts 4:32; 1 Peter 3:8.*
Stand side by side—*Philippians 1:27.*
United in the Holy Spirit—*Ephesians 4:3.*

UNIVERSE

Christ sustains universe—*Colossians 1:17.*
Design of universe proves Designer—
  Romans 1:18-20.
Elohim created universe—*Genesis 1:1.*
Heavens tell of the glory of God—*Psalm 19:1.*

UNPARDONABLE SIN

Blasphemy against Spirit not forgiven—*Mark 3:29,30.*
Sin unto death—*1 John 5:16.*

UNRIGHTEOUSNESS

Every sort of evil—*2 Thessalonians 2:10.*
Godlessness and wickedness—*Romans 1:18.*
Impiety—*Exodus 5:2; 2 Chronicles 32:17; Job 21:14.*
Ungodliness—*2 Timothy 2:16; Titus 2:12; Jude 18.*
Wrongdoing, sin—*1 John 5:17.*

UNSELFISHNESS

Be servant of everyone—*1 Corinthians 9:19.*

Do not be selfish—*Philippians 2:3.*

Do not focus only on your interests—*1 Corinthians 10:24,33; Philippians 2:4.*

Do not just please yourself—*Romans 15:1.*

VANITY

Envy is meaningless (vain)—*Ecclesiastes 4:4*.

Flattering lips and insincere hearts—*Psalm 12:2*.

Pleasure is meaningless (vain)—*Ecclesiastes 2:1*.

Turn eyes from worthless things—*Psalm 119:37*.

Vain boasting—*2 Peter 2:18*.

VEGETATION

Abundant—*Psalm 104:13-15*.

Grass and seed-bearing plants—*Genesis 1:11,29,30*.

Needs rain—*Genesis 2:5*.

Plant a variety of crops—*Ecclesiastes 11:6*.

Plowing and sowing necessary—*Isaiah 28:24*.

VICTORY

Do not lose the race—*Philippians 2:16*.

Fight a good fight—*2 Timothy 4:7*.

In race, one gets prize—*1 Corinthians 9:24*.

Run with endurance—*Hebrews 12:1*.

Strain to reach end of the race—*Philippians 3:14*.

Triumph in Christ—*1 Corinthians 15:57*.

We are more than conquerors—*Romans 8:37*.

VIOLENCE

Acts of violence—*Isaiah 59:6*.

Clothed with violence—*Psalm 73:6*.

Earth filled with violence—*Genesis 6:13*.

Lord, protect me from violent people—*Psalm 140:1*.

VIRGIN BIRTH OF JESUS

Fulfilled—*Matthew 1:23; Luke 1:27.*
Prophesied—*Isaiah 7:14.*

VIRTUE

Fix thoughts on good things—*Philippians 4:8.*
God likes integrity—*1 Chronicles 29:17.*
Live with moral excellence—*2 Peter 1:5.*
Maintain integrity—*Psalm 41:12; Proverbs 11:3; 19:1.*
Manual of integrity—*Book of Proverbs.*
Wisdom and virtue lead to honor—*Proverbs 3:16; 8:18.*

VOW

Be careful in making vow—*Proverbs 20:25.*
Faithfulness required—*Numbers 30:2.*
Nazirite vow—*Numbers 6:2-8.*
Promises to God—*Psalm 76:11.*

WAGES

Do not cheat employees of wages—*Jeremiah 22:13*.
Parable concerning wages—*Matthew 20:1-15*.
Wages of sin is death—*Romans 6:23*.

WAITING

Wait confidently for God—*Micah 7:7*.
Wait for God's mercies—*Psalm 52:9*.
Wait for God's rescue—*Psalm 59:9*.
Wait for Lord's help—*Isaiah 8:17*.
Wait patiently for Lord—*Psalm 27:14; 37:7; 40:1*.
Wait quietly before God—*Psalm 62:1,5*.

WALKING IN GOD'S WAYS

Walk in all God's ways—*Deuteronomy 28:9; Joshua 22:5*.
Walk in the godly way—*Jeremiah 6:16*.
Walk in the Spirit—*Galatians 5:16*.

WAR

Be strong and courageous—*Deuteronomy 31:6*.
Do not war without wise guidance—*Proverbs 24:6*.
End times, many wars—*Matthew 24:6; Mark 13:7*.
God prepares people for battle—*Psalm 18:34*.
God will fight for you—*Exodus 14:14*.

WARDROBE, SPIRITUAL

Be clothed with armor of right living—*Romans 13:12*.
Be clothed with humility—*Colossians 3:12; 1 Peter 5:5,6*.
Be clothed with mercy and love—*Colossians 3:12-14*.

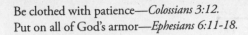

Be clothed with patience—*Colossians 3:12.*
Put on all of God's armor—*Ephesians 6:11-18.*

WATCHFULNESS

Be careful how you live—*Ephesians 5:15.*
Be careful lest you fall—*1 Corinthians 10:12.*
Be careful to love Lord—*Joshua 23:11.*
Be careful to obey—*Joshua 22:5.*
Watch out for attacks from devil—*1 Peter 5:8.*
Watch out, so you do not lose prize—*2 John 8.*
Watch out, you may be seduced—*Job 36:18.*

WATER

God divided sea for Moses—*Exodus 14:21,22.*
Jesus turned water to wine—*John 2:1-11.*
Jesus walked on water—*Matthew 14:25.*

WEAKNESS

Accept Christians weak in faith—*Romans 14:1.*
Disciples cannot bear more teaching—*John 16:12.*
Disciples too weary—*Matthew 26:40.*
God strengthens the weak—*Isaiah 40:29.*
God's strength makes up for our weakness—*2 Corinthians 12:9.*
Spirit strong, body weak—*Matthew 26:41.*

WEALTH

Be trustworthy with worldly wealth—*Luke 16:11.*
False security, wealth—*Jeremiah 49:4.*
Fear of Lord brings wealth—*Proverbs 22:4.*
People who desire wealth fall into temptation—*1 Timothy 6:9,10.*

Weariness

God gives rest to the weary—*Jeremiah 31:25.*

Growing weary in our bodies—*2 Corinthians 5:2.*

We will run and not grow weary—*Isaiah 40:31.*

Weary of living—*Genesis 27:46; Job 3:20.*

Weeping

God will wipe away all tears—*Revelation 7:17.*

Plant in tears, harvest joy—*Psalm 126:5.*

Weeping and gnashing of teeth—*Matthew 8:12; 22:13.*

Wicked

Constant liars—*Proverbs 6:12.*

Far from salvation—*Psalm 119:155.*

From evil people come evil deeds—*1 Samuel 24:13.*

God is angry at the wicked—*Psalm 7:11.*

No peace for the wicked—*Isaiah 57:21.*

Plot against the godly—*Psalm 37:12.*

Punishment of

Calamity will overtake the wicked—*Psalm 34:21.*

Crushed by sins—*Proverbs 14:32.*

Death—*Genesis 2:17; 1 Chronicles 10:13,14.*

Eternal destruction—*Philippians 3:19.*

Lake of Fire—*Revelation 20:15; 21:8.*

Many sorrows—*Psalm 32:10.*

Removed from land—*Proverbs 2:22.*

Sent into everlasting punishment—*Matthew 25:46.*

Shame and disgrace—*Proverbs 13:5.*

Sudden disaster—*Proverbs 24:22.*

Suffer from diseases—*Leviticus 26:16.*

Thrown into fire—*Matthew 13:49,50.*
Years cut short—*Proverbs 10:27.*

WIFE

A treasure—*Proverbs 18:22.*
Husbands must love wives—*Ephesians 5:28.*
Man leaves father and mother, joins wife—
   Genesis 2:24.
Must not leave husband—*1 Corinthians 7:10.*
Must respect husband—*Ephesians 5:33.*
Not good for man to be alone—*Genesis 2:18.*
Submit to husbands—*Ephesians 5:22; Colossians 3:18.*
Virtuous and capable wife—*Proverbs 31:10.*
Wise woman builds her house—*Proverbs 14:1.*
Wives must be respected—*1 Timothy 3:11.*
Woman responsible to husband—*1 Corinthians 11:3.*
Worthy wife is her husband's joy—*Proverbs 12:4.*

WINE

Do not be drunk—*Ephesians 5:18.*
Jesus turned water to wine—*John 2:1-11.*
New wine, old wineskins—*Matthew 9:17; Mark 2:22.*
Wine for medicinal purposes—*1 Timothy 5:23.*

WISDOM

Keep on growing in knowledge—*Philippians 1:9.*
Lord will give you understanding—*2 Timothy 2:7.*
Pray for wisdom—*Psalm 25:4; 27:11; 90:12.*

WITCHCRAFT

Do not consult mediums and psychics—*Leviticus 19:31.*

Execute mediums and psychics—*Leviticus 20:27*.

God is against those who consult mediums—*Leviticus 20:6*.

Medium at Endor—*1 Samuel 28:7-9*.

Sorceress must not be allowed to live—*Exodus 22:18*.

WITNESSES

Complaint against elder requires two or three witnesses—*1 Timothy 5:19*.

More than one needed for death conviction—*Deuteronomy 17:6*.

WOMEN

Be modest in appearance—*1 Timothy 2:9*.

Do not be overly concerned with beauty—*1 Peter 3:3,4*.

God created male and female—*Genesis 1:27*.

Head covered, can prophesy—*1 Corinthians 11:5*.

Keep silent in church—*1 Corinthians 14:34*.

Listen and learn quietly—*1 Timothy 2:11*.

Made from Adam's rib—*Genesis 2:21-23*.

No male or female in Christ—*Galatians 3:28*.

WORD OF GOD

Blessed are those who hear and obey—*Luke 11:28*.

Correctly explain the Word—*2 Timothy 2:15*.

Do not add to or subtract from—*Deuteronomy 4:2*.

Do not distort Word of God—*2 Corinthians 4:2*.

God's Word flawless—*Proverbs 30:5,6*.

God's Word is truth—*John 17:17*.

Jesus' words never pass away—*Matthew 24:35*.

Learn Scriptures from childhood—*2 Timothy 3:15*.

Let word of Christ dwell in you—*Colossians 3:16*.

Love God's Word—*Psalm 119:97-106*.
Word inspired by Holy Spirit—*2 Peter 1:21*.
Word keeps us from sinning—*Psalm 119:9-16*.

WORKS

Good

Be good example, do good deeds—*Titus 2:7*.
Let good deeds shine—*Matthew 5:16*.
We will be judged for good/evil acts—*2 Corinthians 5:10*.

Insufficient for Salvation

No one justified by law—*Romans 3:20*.
Righteous deeds are but filthy rags—*Isaiah 64:6*.
Saved by grace, not works—*Ephesians 2:8,9*.

WORLDLINESS, AVOID

Do not be conformed to world—*Romans 12:2*.
Do not be tied up in affairs of life—*2 Timothy 2:4*.
Do not love praise of men more than God—*John 12:43*.
Do not worry about everyday life—*Matthew 6:25*.
Friendship with world is enmity to God—*James 4:4*.
God's Word can be crowded out by cares of life—
   Matthew 13:22; Luke 8:14.
Set your mind on things above—*Colossians 3:2*.
Stop loving this evil world—*1 John 2:15*.

WORRY

Anxious heart weighs us down—*Proverbs 12:25*.
Cast all anxiety on God—*1 Peter 5:7*.
Do not be anxious about anything—*Philippians 4:6*.
Jesus' advice on anxiety—*Matthew 6:25-34*.

WORSHIP

Lip-service worship is not enough—*Isaiah 29:13.*

Offer your body as a living sacrifice—*Romans 12:1.*

Worship Creator—*Revelation 14:7.*

Worship God with reverence—*Hebrews 12:28.*

Worship in spirit and truth—*John 4:20-24.*

Worship only true God—*Exodus 20:3-5.*

Worship the Lord with gladness—*Psalm 29:2; 100:2.*

Yoke, Figurative

Take my yoke on you—*Matthew 11:29,30.*
Yoke of circumcision—*Acts 15:10.*

Young Men

Do not let people look down on you—*1 Timothy 4:12.*
Encourage young men to live wisely—*Titus 2:6.*
Follow advice—*Proverbs 7:1.*
Prodigal son—*Luke 15:11-32.*
Purity from God's Word—*Psalm 119:9.*
Run from youthful lusts—*2 Timothy 2:22.*

Youth

Do not let anyone despise youth—*1 Timothy 4:12.*
Glory of youth is strength—*Proverbs 20:29.*
Remember creator during youth—*Ecclesiastes 12:1.*
Run from youthful lusts—*2 Timothy 2:22.*

Z

ZEAL

Religious
Be diligent and turn from indifference—*Revelation 3:19*.
Be enthusiastic—*1 Corinthians 15:58*.
Be ready to die for Lord—*Luke 22:33*.
Choose today whom you will serve—*Joshua 24:15*.
Do not put basket over your light—*Mark 4:21*.
Make the most of every opportunity—*Colossians 4:5*.
Never forsake the Lord—*Joshua 24:16*.
Serve the Lord enthusiastically—*Romans 12:11*.
Total commitment—*Titus 2:14*.

Without Knowledge
Apostle Paul prior to conversion—*Galatians 1:13,14*.
Israelites—*Romans 10:2,3*.
Some who preach Christ—*Philippians 1:15*.
Teacher of religious law—*Matthew 8:19,20*.

Other Great Harvest House Books by Ron Rhodes

BOOKS ABOUT ESSENTIAL DOCTRINES

Conviction Without Compromise

Answering the Objections of Atheists, Agnostics, and Skeptics

BOOKS ABOUT THE BIBLE

Commonly Misunderstood Bible Verses

The Book of Bible Promises

The Complete Guide to Bible Translations

What Does the Bible Say About…?

BOOKS ABOUT OTHER RELIGIONS

Find It Quick Handbook on Cults and New Religions

BOOKS ABOUT OTHER IMPORTANT TOPICS

Angels Among Us

The Wonder of Heaven

*The 10 Things You Should Know
About the Creation vs. Evolution Debate*

The Complete Guide to Christian Denominations

The Truth Behind Ghosts, Mediums, and Psychic Phenomena

Northern Storm Rising

The 10 Most Important Things Series
The 10 Most Important Things You Can Say to a Catholic
The 10 Most Important Things You Can Say to a Jehovah's Witness
The 10 Most Important Things You Can Say to a Mormon
The 10 Things You Need to Know About Islam

The Reasoning from the Scriptures Series
Reasoning from the Scriptures with Catholics
Reasoning from the Scriptures with the Jehovah's Witnesses
Reasoning from the Scriptures with the Mormons
Reasoning from the Scriptures with Muslims

Quick Reference Guides
Archaeology and the Bible: What You Need to Know
The Middle East Conflict: What You Need to Know
Halloween: What You Need to Know
Christian Views of War: What You Need to Know
Homosexuality: What You Need to Know
Intelligent Design: What You Need to Know
World Religions: What You Need to Know
Islam: What You Need to Know
Jehovah's Witnesses: What You Need to Know